The ANGLER'S GUIDE to
FRESHWATER FISH
≈ of NORTH AMERICA ≈

Eric L. Sorenson

Voyageur Press

Edited by Danielle J. Ibister
Designed by Kristy Tucker
Printed in China

00   01   02   03   04   5   4   3   2   1

Library of Congress Cataloging-in-Publication Data
Sorenson, Eric L., 1966-
     The angler's guide to freshwater fish of North America / Eric L. Sorenson.
          p. cm.
     Includes bibliographical references.
     ISBN 0-89658-463-1
     1. Freshwater fishes—North America. 2. Fishing—North America. I. Title.
     QL625.S67 2000
     597.176'0973—dc21
                                                          99-044855

Distributed in Canada by Raincoast Books, 8680 Cambie Street, Vancouver, B.C. V6P 6M9

Published by Voyageur Press, Inc.
123 North Second Street, P.O. Box 338, Stillwater, MN 55082 U.S.A.
651-430-2210, fax 651-430-2211

Educators, fundraisers, premium and gift buyers, publicists, and marketing managers: Looking for creative products and new sales ideas? Voyageur Press books are available at special discounts when purchased in quantities, and special editions can be created to your specifications. For details contact the marketing department at 800-888-9653.

Page 1: *Each day on the river or lake brings new adventure to North America's freshwater anglers. Whether fishing for coho salmon in Alaska, largemouth bass in Florida, brook trout in Maine, striped bass in California, or catfish somewhere in between, anglers always hope their next catch will surpass previous ones in beauty and size.* Photograph © Bill Buckley/The Green Agency

Page 4: *Bluegills and other sunfish are among the most abundant and recognizable game fish in North America's freshwaters. Sunfish tolerate a wide range of habitats and climates, and adapt well to transplantation in nonnative waters. They are prolific, resistant, and often thrive where more habitat-sensitive species perish.* Photograph © Larry Mishkar/PictureSmith

The freshwaters of North America offer diverse game fish. Some, like the rainbow trout, are familiar and available to many anglers. Others are rare, obscure, and remote, roaming the lakes and rivers of our continent in virtual anonymity, known only to small segments of the angling community. Photograph © Bill Buckley/The Green Agency

Dedication

To my grandfather, Grant Suiter, for introducing me to the joys of fishing, and to my parents, Lowell and Judy Sorenson, for their support and encouragement.

Acknowledgments

The author wishes to thank the National Fresh Water Fishing Hall of Fame and the Minnesota Department of Natural Resources.

CONTENTS

OUR FISHING TRADITION

I was introduced to the sport of fishing by my grandpa, who helped me catch my first yellow perch when I was three years old. At that point in his life, Grandpa still enjoyed catching fish, but it brought him even greater joy to see me, his grandson—a symbol of a new generation of anglers—reeling in a fish. Through my early years, Grandpa taught me all he knew about fish and fishing and answered my endless string of questions about the sport. I remember many a hot summer day spent on the lakes of northern Minnesota, talking, and waiting for fish to bite.

When I am out on a lake or stream today, more than thirty years after I caught my first fish, I see grandfathers and fathers teaching the next generation of anglers about fishing and my mind replays those summer days with my grandpa, who passed away twenty years ago. Fishing is like that: It binds generations with irreplaceable memories. In North America fishing is a tradition. Whether an angler learns the sport from a family member, or just picks it up on his or her own, that individual is carrying on a long-standing tradition.

Like all traditions, the sport of fishing has evolved to meet the needs of the present. When the first European settlers arrived in North America more than half a millennium ago, the distribution of the continent's game fish was different than today. There were no brook trout in the Rocky Mountains, no largemouth bass in California, no chinook salmon in the Great Lakes, no striped bass in inland waters, and no brown trout anywhere on the continent. Over the centuries, first anglers and then fisheries' managers transplanted the continent's favorite game fish

❦

Today's young anglers represent the future of fishing in North America. Parents, grandparents, aunts, and uncles who introduce children to the riches of angling set the foundation for a new generation of appreciation and respect for the continent's fish and the sport of fishing. Research shows children introduced to angling by age ten are more likely to grow into lifelong anglers than kids introduced to the sport at later ages. Photograph © Rob & Ann Simpson

The freshwaters of North America are as diverse and beautiful as the game fish species that inhabit them. Whether fishing on a small neighborhood pond or a rugged mountain lake, the serenity of escape is often as compelling as the thrill of a striking fish. Photograph © Jeff Henry/Roche Jaune Pictures, Inc.

to new waters and created fisheries to meet the demands of the sport fishing community. Some five hundred years later, North America has entirely different fishing opportunities and a wide spectrum of game fish from which to choose.

As the scope of our angling opportunities has evolved, so have the attitudes of our fishermen and women. Quickly disappearing is the catch-and-kill attitude of generations past. Anglers are learning rapidly that North America's game fish resources are finite and fragile. There are species that have suffered from years of overharvesting and habitat destruction. The hard work of fisheries' managers and nonprofit organizations have repaired the damage in many cases, but some damage is irreparable, and new dangers continue to arise, threatening the delicate balance of North America's fisheries.

One hundred years from now, when the great-grandchildren of today's young anglers continue the tradition of fishing in North America's freshwaters, the face of angling will have changed once again. It is our duty to instill in new generations a respect for the fish they seek. We must protect this priceless resource—assuring future anglers the same pleasures we have known out on the freshwaters of our continent—fishing.

Chapter 1

BLACK BASS

As the sport of fishing has grown and evolved in North America, one group of game fish has risen to the top to become the continent's premier species. Members of this group are collectively referred to as black bass. A variety of factors, including range, accessibility, adaptability, and a host of physical traits, have contributed to black bass gaining an unparalleled following in North America. Today, no group of game fish is more sought after in such a vast area—from the Great Lakes to the Gulf of Mexico, and from the Pacific to Atlantic coasts.

Because anglers hold black bass, specifically the largemouth bass, in such high esteem, no world record game fish has a bigger bull's-eye on it, or carries more mystique, than the 22-pound, 4-ounce (10.09 kg) largemouth bass caught by George W. Perry at Montgomery Lake, Georgia, in 1932. Although millions of anglers have tried to break his record, few have landed largemouth anywhere near the size of Perry's epic catch.

Powerful, feisty, and aggressive, black bass are not really bass at all. They are members of the sunfish, *Centrarchidae*, family, which includes thirty species of fish. Black bass belong to the *Micropterus* genus, which boasts the largest species in the sunfish family.

Tenacity, strength, beauty, and size—all important game fish characteristics—have helped propel black bass to their current standing; however, range is another key factor in their popularity. Native to parts of the central, eastern, and southeastern

~✦~

The largemouth bass has stolen the hearts of millions of North America's anglers. Each year the largemouth draws flocks of new anglers to ponds, lakes, and rivers. Some believe the largemouth is the perfect game fish: strong, tough, resistant, and alluring—a pure, natural fighter that never gives up. For loyal largemouth bass fishermen and women, landing a trophy largemouth is the ultimate angling experience. Photograph © Doug Stamm/ProPhoto

United States, and south-central Canada, the black bass's ranges have expanded to include most of the United States, northern Mexico, and southern Canada.

Although largemouth and smallmouth bass often overshadow other black bass species, in regions of the south-central and southeastern United States, the spotted, redeye, Guadalupe, Suwannee, and shoal bass play important roles in the game fish communities.

Black bass are, as any angler who has caught one knows, not really black. Most are dark green with a whitish undersurface, have dark markings on the side, and a black spot at the back of the gill cover. They have large mouths, with jaws extending to or beyond the eye. The body is fairly long and slightly compressed from the sides. They have between nine and eleven spines on their dorsal fins and fifty-five or more lateral scales.

Like most sunfish species, black bass spawn in the spring. The males make the nests, and will then guard the eggs and newly hatched fry.

Their habitat ranges from clear rock-bottomed lakes and streams to murky ponds and backwaters of rivers.

LARGEMOUTH BASS

Much of black bass's popularity stems from the North American freshwater anglers' love affair with the largemouth bass, *Micropterus salmoides*, which has become the most popular and widespread species on the continent.

The largemouth's native range stretched from Minnesota to southern Quebec in the North, and from Texas to Florida in the South. During the nineteenth and twentieth centuries, the largemouth's range swelled due to extensive transplantation. The fish's adaptability and prolificacy allowed planting in a wide spectrum of waters. Today its range includes most of the United States, northern Mexico, and much of southern Canada.

The largemouth's accessibility is one factor in its popularity, but its reputation as a powerful and aggressive predator is what keeps anglers going back to ponds, lakes, and rivers to pursue it.

As a predator, the largemouth is an efficient and potent killer. This fish has, as its name implies, an exceptionally large mouth, which it uses to devour a variety of prey ranging from fish and insects to mice, frogs, salamanders, and even ducklings. Its extended, laterally compressed body allows it to maneuver in tight areas and move with short bursts of speed to nab prey.

Although sight is its most important sense in finding and attacking prey, the largemouth also depends on its heightened sense of feel along its lateral lines. These narrow lines run along the sides of its body from head to tail and allow the largemouth to feel vibrations in the water and key in on potential prey. Largemouth that live in murky waters, where prey is not easily seen, depend more on their sense of feel to find food. Studies show even blindfolded largemouths can catch minnows with the help of their lateral lines.

An important aspect of a quality largemouth bass habitat is the presence of aquatic plants. Without dense plant growth, the largemouth loses much of its advantage in finding food and avoiding predators. Adults lurk among aquatic plants waiting to pounce on unsuspecting prey, while young largemouths use these plants as safe refuges from predators. Photograph © Larry Mishkar/PictureSmith

In relation to body size, the largemouth bass has the largest mouth of any game fish in North America's freshwaters. The fish's enormous mouth allows it to attack and devour a variety of prey, ranging from small fish and insects to mice and ducklings. The largemouth's tenacious temperament, willingness to strike a variety of prey, and vast distribution have built a following of anglers unparalleled by any other fish on the continent. Photograph © Doug Stamm/ProPhoto

While the largemouth depends greatly on its senses to find food, its markings also play an important role in catching prey, as well as in hiding from predators. Colored dark green above and white below, with a black stripe running along its brassy-green side, the largemouth is an expert at camouflage. Its dark colors on top make it difficult to see against the dark floor below, and its light coloring underneath keeps it camouflaged against the daylight from above. As a largemouth's surroundings change, so do its colors. In clear, shallow water, its colors tend to be bright and definite; in dark or murky water, its colors are drab.

In addition to affecting its coloring, a largemouth's environment also influences the fish's growth rate and the length of its life. Although a largemouth can tolerate temperatures from near freezing to 95°F, its ideal temperature range for growth is in the 80s (27°C to 32°C). Thus, a largemouth living in Minnesota's cold climate, where the yearly growing period is four to five months, does not grow as quickly as a largemouth living in Georgia's mild climate, where temperatures are in the ideal range for up to eight months. However, this equation does not necessarily mean the Georgia largemouth will grow larger over the course of its lifetime, because largemouths in northern waters typically live at least five years longer. The exception is the Florida subspecies, *Micropterus salmoides floridanus*, native to the panhandle of Florida; this fish, which accounts for many of the largemouths weighing 15 pounds (6.8 kg) or more, is genetically capable of growing much larger than its northern cousins.

Gender also affects a largemouth's size and longevity. Females typically live three to five years more than males and tend to grow larger. Few female largemouths in the South live to age ten, but they can live as long as fifteen years in the North.

Spawning

Life for the largemouth begins in the spring. When the water temperature approaches 60°F (16°C), mature largemouths ages three and up move to the spawning grounds. The male arrives at the spawning area first, selecting a nesting area in water less than 6 feet (1.8 m) deep, and over a firm sandy or silty bottom. He either builds a circular nest by fanning his fins over the bottom or selects a vacant nest or a clear spot on the bottom. When the water temperature reaches 63°F to 68°F (17°C to 20°C), he coerces a ripe female to the nest. A 5-pound (2.3-kg) female can lay as many as thirty-five thousand eggs. When fertilization is complete, the male remains on the nest to guard the eggs from predators, while the female moves away from the spawning area into deeper water to recuperate.

Once hatched, the fry form a school and feed on tiny zooplankton and crustaceans. The adult male continues its vigilant watch, forsaking food to guard the young. When the fry have grown to about 1 inch (2.5 cm) in length they leave the nest and the male begins feeding again. If food is in short supply, the adult male may eat the young he has spent all his time and energy guarding, or he may feed on fry from another nest.

When the young largemouths reach fingerling size, they eat larger

During much of largemouth bass season, anglers concentrate their efforts during the early morning and evening hours, the fish's peak feeding times. Between dusk and dawn, largemouths are often found in shallow water, but during the day, especially in summer, they move out to deeper water. Photograph © Jack Bissell

crustaceans and insects. Eventually they will prey on minnows and invertebrates.

Habitat

Although more than one are commonly found in a given area of a lake or river, the largemouth is a solitary fish. When found in a group, they are not schooling; rather, they are together because the same food or habitat has brought them to the same place.

The largemouth seeks out quiet water, usually less than 20 feet (5 m) deep, with plenty of cover. Heavy aquatic weeds and submerged trees, logs, or brush are common hiding places. In rivers, they live away from the main current, preferring calm backwaters or pools.

Despite being able to tolerate water temperatures up to 95°F (35°C), the largemouth favors cool to warm water. When water temperatures rise during the summer months, the largemouth moves to deeper, shaded water where temperatures are more stable, though the fish usually does not travel very far beyond the weedline. It comes into heated shallow water to feed in the evening and remains there until morning. As the water cools in the fall, the largemouth will spend more time in shallow water, usually 10 feet (3 m) or less in depth. During the winter, it will move back to deeper water in search of stable temperatures, prey, and—in lakes with ice cover—oxygen.

During the winter in its northern range, where bitter cold freezes the surfaces of lakes and rivers and water temperatures hover just above the freezing point, the largemouth remains mostly inactive. Body functions slow to near hibernation levels, and a month or more may pass before the fish feeds.

SMALLMOUTH BASS

Although it has not received the acclaim or the widespread stocking of its cousin the largemouth, the smallmouth bass, *Mircropterus dolomieu*, is still one of North America's favorite game fish.

The smallmouth's native range was bound by an area stretching from western North Dakota to southern Quebec in the North, and from eastern Oklahoma to western North Carolina in the South. Like the largemouth, its range has increased through transplantation, but the smallmouth is not as adaptable as its cousin, so its range is not as expansive. Today, the smallmouth is found across much of the United States and southern Canada. Unlike the largemouth, its range does not extend to Florida or Louisiana.

Like other black bass, the smallmouth is a strong, efficient predator, valued by anglers for its aggressive nature and impressive appearance.

Although the smallmouth has a shorter jaw than the largemouth, it still has a fairly large mouth, especially suited for picking crayfish out of rock crevices, and catching other prey like fish, insects, and frogs.

The smallmouth's elongated, laterally compact body is colored bronze-brown to olive green on the top and on the sides, and grayish-white below, with dark brown bars running vertically down its sides.

The smallmouth bass is more susceptible to overfishing than the largemouth, due in part to habitat. Smallmouths often inhabit shallow streams that offer good angling access, while largemouths lives in lakes with deeper water and more cover. Another factor is abundance: The density of the smallmouth's population in a lake or stream is usually far lower than that of the largemouth's, which means angling pressure that is tolerable in a largemouth lake or stream could quickly overfish a smallmouth body of water. Photograph © Doug Stamm/ProPhoto

The smallmouth's colors change to blend with its habitat. When hiding among dark surroundings like rocks or submerged branches, its colors are dark; in dirty water, its colors are lighter and more yellow.

Although the smallmouth, especially compared to the largemouth, is not an exceptionally large fish, it is larger than some of its other black bass cousins, which contributes to its popularity. An average smallmouth weighs 1 to 3 pounds (.45 to 1.4 kg). The world record smallmouth caught by John T. Gorman at Dale Hollow Lake, Tennessee, in 1969, weighed 10 pounds, 14 ounces (4.93 kg)—half the size of the record largemouth, but still an impressive fish.

Spawning

In the spring, when water temperatures approach the low 60s (16°C to 21°C), both the male and female adults begin moving toward the spawning grounds, found over gravel in the shallows of a lake or in quiet areas of a river or stream. The male moves in first to make a nest. Next to the largemouth bass, who is a comparatively sloppy nest builder, the smallmouth male is scrupulous in his nest building. Working for a day or more, he fans out a clean, circular area measuring about 2 feet (60 cm) in diameter. When he is finished, he brings a female to the nest to spawn. A female lays anywhere from two thousand to twenty thousand eggs, depending on her size. The adhesive eggs stick to the nest's gravel, where they lay for three to ten days before hatching.

Like the largemouth, the smallmouth male remains on the nest, guarding the eggs from intruders. He also fans the eggs to keep them clear of any silt buildup. The female abandons the nesting area in search of deeper water where she can recuperate.

Newly hatched fry remain on the nest for a week or two, feeding on their yolk sac. When the fry have grown to about an inch in length, the male leaves in search of food and the fry must fend for themselves.

Habitat

Unlike the largemouth, which adapts to a wide variety of habitat conditions and water temperatures, the smallmouth requires a more specific environment. It prefers clear, moving water with a gravel or rock bottom. Although smallmouths do thrive in many lakes and reservoirs, they are more commonly found in cool, clear streams and rivers with moderate flows. Still water may not provide the dissolved oxygen the smallmouth requires, while rushing white water may be too stressful an environment.

The smallmouth typically chooses hiding places like rocks, boulders, and submerged tree limbs, which are ideal for ambushing prey. In rivers, it seeks areas where fast and slow waters converge, like the back or head of a pool or an eddy, waiting for food to come to it.

The smallmouth tolerates water temperatures ranging from near freezing to the mid-80s (28°C to 31°C), but its ideal growing temperature range is the 70s (21°C to 26°C). Temperatures approaching 90°F (32°C) are deadly—one reason the smallmouth's range does not extend

A common nickname for the small-mouth bass is bronzeback, which refers to the bronze or brassy tint of the fish's back and sides. As light changes within its habitat, the degree of its coloring changes quickly, fading in direct sunlight and darkening in low light. Photograph © Bill Buckley/The Green Agency

into the deep South.

During its active periods in the spring, summer, and fall, the small-mouth spends much of its time in cool, shallow water. As temperatures rise in the heart of summer, the fish spends most of its time in water up to 20 feet (5 m) in depth, where the temperatures are more stable, and comes into shallow water in the evening to feed, remaining there until morning.

As winter approaches and temperatures fall, the smallmouth migrates to its winter resting place, where it remains largely inactive. In a stream, its winter site may be a larger river or a deep pool within a stream; in a lake, the site is usually deeper, warmer water.

SPOTTED BASS

Colored dark green above and white below, with a black vertical line running from head to tail, the spotted or Kentucky bass, *Micropterus punctulatus*, bears a striking resemblance to the largemouth bass. Its dark line though, is more a series of connected large, black spots than a continuous line. It also has vertical rows of smaller black spots running along the lower half of its body, thus the name "spotted" bass. Its mouth is not as large, coming closer to the size of a smallmouth's.

The spotted bass's native range stretched from southwestern Nebraska to southern Ohio and central West Virginia in the North, and from southeastern Texas to the panhandle of Florida in the South. Its range has expanded due to stocking to include other parts of Texas, Missouri, Virginia, Colorado, New Mexico, and California, but it cannot claim the territory of either the largemouth or smallmouth.

Genetically, the spotted bass's closest relative in the black bass family is the smallmouth, but it does not grow as large as its cousin. The world record spotted bass weighed more than 9 pounds (4 kg), but a typical adult weighs between 1 and 2 pounds (.45 to .9 kg). The spotted bass also has a shorter life span than the smallmouth and rarely lives past age six.

The spotted bass prefers clear streams and rivers with gravel bottoms, but also occupies the deep waters of reservoirs. Although a cool-water fish, the spotted bass cannot tolerate prolonged periods of water temperatures in the 30s (−1°C to 4°C) or areas where lakes or rivers freeze over for many months; thus it does not live in northern states such as Michigan, Minnesota, and Wisconsin.

In streams, the spotted bass spends the spring, summer, and fall in shallow pools and flows. As winter approaches it will move downstream to deeper pools, in search of warmer water. In the spring, it moves back upstream in preparation for the spawn. Spotted bass that live in reservoirs spend most of their time in water between 20 and 30 feet (5 and 6 m) deep.

Crayfish make up a large part of the spotted bass's diet, along with small fish and insects. Much of the spotted bass's feeding time is spent picking crayfish out of rocky areas. A specially adapted patch of teeth on the fish's tongue make it efficient at eating these crustaceans.

Three subspecies of spotted bass roam the waters of the United States: the northern spotted bass, Micropterus punctulatus punctulatus; *the Alabama spotted bass,* Micropterus punctulatus henshalli; *and the Wichita spotted bass,* Micropterus punctulatus wichitae. *Like the largemouth and smallmouth bass, the spotted bass is highly prized by anglers, though it does not grow as fast or as large as either cousin. In its first year of life, the spotted bass grows to 1½ to 4 inches (3.8–10 cm). The fish reaches maturity in its second or third year, when it measures approximately 7 inches (18 cm). The spotted bass's closest relative in the black bass family is the Guadalupe bass. The two species are similar in appearance, but the Guadalupe bass has dark bars on its sides while the spotted bass does not.* Photograph © Keith Sutton

~ CRAYFISH ~

*T*he crayfish—known regionally as the crawfish or crawdad—is a major source of food for black bass and other game fish. This small freshwater crustacean can be found across the entire United States, much of Canada, and sections of Mexico. The approximately 100 different crayfish species in North America average 2 to 5 inches (5 cm to 13 cm) in length and vary in color from brown to blue. Smallmouth and spotted bass feed heavily on the lobster-like creature, which makes up as much as 50 percent of the fish's diet in some waters.

Crayfish live in shallow water amidst rocks, submerged logs, and mud burrows of rivers, streams, lakes, ponds, and swamps. They remain hidden in the safety of their chosen cover during the day, then venture out at night in search of food. Scavengers, crayfish prey on dead fish, minnows, fish eggs, plants, and other aquatic creatures.

Many anglers bait their lines with live crayfish or crayfish tails. In some parts of the United States, crayfish are harvested also for human consumption.

Crayfish are a favored food of black bass. The spotted, Suwannee, and redeye bass are equipped with special patches of teeth on their tongue that help crush the crayfish's tough shell. In some parts of their range, more than half of a black bass's diet consists of crayfish.
Photograph © Doug Stamm/ProPhoto

SUWANNEE BASS

Named for the river that constitutes much of its North American range, the Suwannee bass, *Micropterus notius*, is one of the rarest members of the black bass family. Its range is limited to the small rivers and backwater streams of the Suwannee and Ochlockonee River drainages of southern Georgia and northern Florida.

The Suwannee's body is not as laterally compact as other black bass. Its colors are dark green above and light below, with dark markings on a greenish-brown side. The adult male commonly has a turquoise breast, belly, and cheeks. The Suwannee is small compared to other black bass. The world record, caught by Laverne Norton in 1984 at the Ochlockonee River, weighed 3 pounds, 9 ounces (1.62 kg).

Like the spotted bass, the Suwannee has a patch of teeth on its tongue that serves as an efficient tool for eating crayfish. It also feeds on insects, frogs, and small fish.

First identified as a distinct black bass species in 1949, the Suwannee bass has been designated a "species of special concern" in recognition of its limited range and distribution. Because it rarely grows in excess of 1 pound (.45 kg), the Suwannee does not receive the same angler attention as its larger cousins. Photograph © Doug Stamm/ProPhoto

The redeye bass, pictured here, and its cousin the shoal bass are similar in appearance and size. An easy way to tell the two apart is to check the tongue: The redeye bass has a patch of teeth on its tongue, while the shoal bass does not. Another clue is found on the tail fin: Both fish have reddish tail fins, but the redeye bass has white outer edges on its tail fin. A more time-consuming means of distinguishing between the two species is to count their lateral scales: The redeye bass typically has between sixty-four and seventy-three lateral scales, while the shoal bass usually has seventy to seventy-nine. Photograph © Richard T. Bryant

Because populations are low in much of its range, the Suwannee's harvest is restricted to help assure its protection.

GUADALUPE BASS

Like the Suwannee, the Guadalupe bass, *Micropterus treculi*, has a limited range. Its populations are indigenous to an area of central Texas that includes drainages of the Brazos, Colorado, Guadalupe, and San Antonio Rivers. It was introduced to parts of the Nueces River drainage in the same region.

The Guadalupe's closest relative is the spotted bass. Its colors are dark above and light below, with dark bars running vertically down its sides. The Guadalupe usually weighs less than its closest cousin: While the spotted bass averages 1 to 2 pounds (.45 kg to .9 kg), the Guadalupe averages less than 1 pound (.45 kg). The world record weighed just under 4 pounds (1.8 kg).

The Guadalupe bass is found in creeks and small rivers. It prefers gravel-bottom runs and pools where it feeds on small fish, insects, and crayfish.

REDEYE BASS

Distinguishable by its red fins, the redeye bass, *Micropterus coosae*, is another black bass species that inhabits a relatively small range. Its native range includes parts of the Chattahoochee, Mobile Bay, and Savannah basins from northern Alabama to western South Carolina. Its range has expanded through stocking to include parts of Kentucky, Georgia, and California.

The redeye's colorings are dark green to olive above and yellowish-white below, though it can take on a bluish tint to its breast and belly. Dark patches, less distinct than those on its cousins, run along its brassy-green side. The redeye is small compared to other black bass species: The average redeye weighs about 1 pound (.45 kg); the world record weighed less than 4 pounds (1.8 kg).

The redeye prefers a habitat of running water. It usually lives in the pools and runs of gravel or rock-bottomed streams and rivers. Like the spotted and Suwannee bass, the redeye uses a patch of teeth on its tongue to eat crayfish. The redeye also feeds on insects and small fish.

SHOAL BASS

A very close cousin of the redeye bass is the shoal bass. Its sparse populations live in a range limited to the drainages of the Apalachicola River system along the Alabama/Georgia border and the panhandle of Florida.

Like the redeye, the shoal is dark green to olive above and light below, with red fins. However, it has more distinct dark, vertical markings on its brassy-green side. Like the redeye, the shoal's average size is about 1 pound (.45 kg), yet the world record weighed more than 8 pounds (3.6 kg). The shoal bass inhabits the pools and runs of rocky flows in streams and rivers, where it feeds on small fish, insects, worms, and crayfish.

Chapter 2

PANFISH

T he childhood experience of seeing that very first fish wiggling at the end of a line is a memory an angler never forgets. For some, it was a catfish, for others, a yellow perch, but most anglers are proud to say the first fish they caught was a sunfish. It was probably caught while fishing from shore, or from their father's or grandfather's boat on a pond, lake, or river near home. The fishing rod was most likely an old cane pole or starter spinning rod. The bait was no doubt a worm, grasshopper, or minnow suspended underneath a bobber. Those same anglers still fish for sunfish every once in a while, just because they are fun to catch.

Sunfish and their cousins—the crappies, rock bass, and warmouth—belong to the *Centrarchidae* family, which also includes black bass. North America's waters teem with these cooperative, scrappy, prolific, great-tasting little fish, so it's no wonder they are among the continent's most popular game fish species.

There are about ten sunfish and crappie species common to large sections of the United States and southern Canada. They are known by countless different names throughout their widespread range, so it is not uncommon for anglers to confuse one species with another.

Often painted in a palette of dramatic colors, sunfish rank near the top of North America's list of most beautiful game fish. One would think their colorful markings would make them easy to identify, but more often, sunfish species are difficult to distinguish from one another. Many species are similar in appearance, but markings vary from region to region.

The pumpkinseed, one of the most colorful freshwater game fish in North America, is also one of the continent's most common sunfish species. The pumpkinseed was originally limited to waters east of the Mississippi River, but, thanks to extensive transplantation, it is now found as far west as California. Photograph © Doug Stamm/ProPhoto

To make things more difficult, different species often spawn with one another, creating some confusing hybrids.

Most sunfish belong to the *Lepomis* genus. They are characterized by their disk-shaped, laterally compressed bodies. They have two dorsal fins that, at first glance, appear to be one long fin; the first has sharp spines and the second has soft rays. Their mouths usually are small and often bear tiny teeth. Other common characteristics include a dark spot on the ear cover, a mildly forked tail, and fewer than fifty-five lateral scales.

On average, sunfish live five to six years. An exceptionally old sunfish reaches age eight or nine. Most sunfish reach sexual maturity between the ages of one and three.

Sunfish are warm-water species that adapt well to various habitat conditions. In the South, they tolerate the warm water of summer; in the North, they can withstand prolonged, frigid winters. Sunfish usually congregate in shallow water in ponds, lakes, streams, or rivers. They take cover among heavy weeds, submerged trees, rocks, or other structures where they search out food such as insects, invertebrates, and small fish. As much as 85 percent of a sunfish's diet consists of insects.

Sunfish spawn in the spring or summer when the water temperature is between 67°F and 80°F (10°C and 27°C). When temperatures reach this optimal range, the male builds a nest in shallow water, usually less than 3 feet (90 cm) deep, over a firm bottom. By fanning his fins he creates a circular bed for the eggs. He then coerces a female to the nest for spawning. Depending on her size, she may lay as many as fifty thousand adhesive eggs that stick to the bottom of the nest. After the male fertilizes the eggs, the female leaves the nesting area to recuperate from her exhausting activity. The male remains on the nest to guard the eggs. When the fry hatch, he guards them for a few days before leaving the nesting area to resume feeding. This attentive parental care is one reason sunfish are such prolific species.

When the fry hatch, they school and feed on tiny zooplankton. As they grow larger, the fish are able to feed on insects and invertebrates.

BLUEGILL

North America's most popular and widespread sunfish species is the bluegill, *Lepomis macrochirus*. The name derives from the bright bluish head and gill cover of the breeding male. The rest of his body is dark green above, yellow to orange on the belly with a bright orange breast, and dark vertical bars on his sides. Older males develop a purplish tinge throughout their body. Females, dark green above and green to white on the sides and belly, lack the impressive colors of the male.

The bluegill is one of the largest sunfish found in North America. The average bluegill weighs about ½ pound (.23 kg), though larger specimens are common in the South. The world record caught by T. S. Hudson at Ketona Lake, Alabama, in 1950, weighed 4 pounds, 12 ounces (2.15 kg).

Originally inhabiting a range that stretched from eastern South Dakota

to Quebec in the North, and from northern Mexico to Florida in South, the bluegill's range has expanded dramatically from transplantation. Today, it inhabits all forty-eight of the contiguous states and much of southern Canada.

The bluegill's habitat includes weedy lakes, ponds, slow-moving streams, and the backwaters of rivers. Less tolerant of low oxygen levels than many of its cousins, the bluegill is commonly a victim of winterkill. During the spring and summer, the bluegill may spawn as many as three times, which is a key factor in its prolificacy and abundant presence in North American waters.

With the right combination of food, cover, quality spawning grounds, and predators, bluegills grow quickly and occasionally reach weights in excess of 2 pounds (.9 kg). However, when habitat conditions are not ideal, bluegills can overpopulate a water body. A high population, few predators, and an inadequate food supply contribute to a stunted bluegill population in which few ever reach 1 pound (.45 kg). Photograph © William H. Mullins

PUMPKINSEED

One of the most dramatically colored sunfish is the pumpkinseed, *Lepomis gibbosus*. The male has a flaming gold lower half and iridescent blue-green and yellow specks on its upper half. Its head and gill cover are streaked with blue lightning bolt-like lines, and the dark spot on its ear cover has a bright orange edge. The female's coloring is similar, but tends to be more drab and washed out than the male's.

Although pumpkinseeds are capable of growing nearly as large as the bluegill, they are usually smaller. Their average size is between ¼ and ½ pound (.11 and .23 kg).

The pumpkinseed's native range covered an area from southeastern Manitoba to New Brunswick in the North, and from northern Missouri

An average pumpkinseed weighs less than ½ pound (.23 kg), but these scrappy sunfish grow over 1 pound (.45 kg) in ideal habitat conditions. The world record, caught by Scott Hart at North Saluda River, South Carolina, in 1997, weighed 2 pounds, 4 ounces (1.02 kg). Photograph © Rob & Ann Simpson

to South Carolina in the South. Widespread introduction has extended the pumpkinseed's range as far west as the Pacific Coast in the United States and Canada.

Like other sunfish, the pumpkinseed feeds heavily on insects and invertebrates, but it also favors snails. Its unique teeth, which are located in the throat, help it efficiently break up the snail's hard shell.

The pumpkinseed commonly lives alongside the bluegill. It prefers weedy lakes, ponds, the pools of streams, and the backwaters of rivers.

Like the bluegill, the pumpkinseed often spawns more than once in a season, contributing to its abundance. In a single summer, a female may produce more than fifteen thousand offspring.

GREEN SUNFISH

A large mouth, stocky body, and plain colors make the green sunfish, *Lepomis cyanellus*, one of the easiest sunfish to identify. Named for its dominant color, the green sunfish is dark green to blue-green above and yellow below, with green vertical bars on its sides. It has green wavy lines

The green sunfish is less selective about its food sources than sunfish like the redear and pumpkinseed. The green sunfish feeds on a wide variety of minnows, aquatic and terrestrial insects, frogs, and crayfish. Its willingness to eat just about anything that fits in its mouth supports the green sunfish's reputation as one of the most aggressive members of the sunfish family. Photograph © Patrice Ceisel/Shedd Aquarium

or flecks on its gill cover, and the dark spot on its ear cover has a white edge. Although the world record weighed more than 2 pounds (.9 kg), green sunfish commonly weigh less than ½ pound (.23 kg).

The green sunfish originally inhabited a range stretching from southern Ontario and Minnesota to western New York in the North, and from northern Mexico to the panhandle of Florida in the South. Its range expanded due to stocking to include much of the United States and southern Canada, including parts of the Pacific Coast.

Like other sunfish species, the green sunfish lives in weedy lakes, ponds, slow-moving streams, and the backwaters of rivers. It can, however, withstand warmer, murkier, and more turbid water than its cousins, and is better able to cope with lower oxygen levels.

In contrast to more prolific sunfish species such as the bluegill and pumpkinseed, the green sunfish usually spawns just once a season.

LONGEAR SUNFISH

Often confused with the pumpkinseed, the longear sunfish, *Lepomis megalotis*, is one of the most brilliantly colored sunfish species. Named for it's long ear flap, which distinguishes it from the pumpkinseed, the longear sunfish is flecked with red, gold, and green-blue above and on the sides, and is gold to orange below. Like the pumpkinseed, its head and gill cover are streaked with wavy blue lines. The average longear weighs less than ½ pound (.23 kg). The world record, caught by Patricia Stout at Elephant Butte Lake, New Mexico, in 1985, weighed 1 pound, 12 ounces (.79 kg).

The longear's native range extended from southwestern Ontario and northern Minnesota to western New York in the North, and from northern Mexico to the Florida panhandle in the South. Though introduced to numerous areas outside its native range, the longear does not inhabit as many waters as the bluegill, pumpkinseed, or green sunfish.

In contrast to the majority of sunfish species, the longear most commonly lives in streams and rivers and is unlikely to inhabit lakes and ponds.

The Greek term megalotis *in the longear sunfish's scientific name means "great ear" and refers to the fish's long ear covers, which are especially evident in breeding-age males. The longear's ear covers, with their flexible edges, help distinguish it from the pumpkinseed, which has short ear covers with rigid edges.* Photograph © Mark Giovanetti/ProPhoto

ORANGESPOTTED SUNFISH

Although beautifully colored, the orangespotted sunfish, *Lepomis humilis*, does not receive much attention from anglers because of its size. An average orangespotted sunfish weighs about ¼ pound, and even the largest rarely weigh more than ½ pound (.23 kg).

The orangespotted sunfish is colored dark green above and orange to red below, with silvery-blue flecks and orange spots on its sides. Its head is blue to silver with wavy orange to red lines.

Originally inhabiting a range stretching from southern North Dakota to Ohio in the North, and from western Texas to Alabama in the South, the orangespotted sunfish's range has expanded due to stocking. Its ability to tolerate more polluted water than other sunfish species has allowed it to persist where its cousins have perished.

The orangespotted sunfish more commonly lives in creeks and rivers than in lakes or ponds.

REDEAR SUNFISH

One of the largest sunfish species is the redear sunfish, *Lepomis microlophus*. The world record weighed nearly 5 pounds (2.3 kg), but an average redear weighs about ¾ pound (.34 kg). Lacking the brilliant colors of most sunfish, the redear is colored light green above and white to yellow below, with gray spots on its sides. One of its distinguishing features is the orange outer edge of its ear cover's dark spot.

Although the orangespotted sunfish is one of the most colorful of the sunfish species, anglers pay little attention to this small fish. A ¼-pound (.11-kg) orangespotted sunfish is large, and anything approaching ½ pound (.23 kg) is worthy of mounting. Few states even keep records for orangespotted sunfish, though Tennessee boasts a state record of 5.44 ounces (.15 kg). Photograph © Patrice Ceisel/Shedd Aquarium

33

Redear sunfish typically live in deeper water than sunfish species like the bluegill or pumpkinseed. Redears are drawn to structures such as logs, roots, stumps, and aquatic plants. It is a difficult sunfish to catch because it shies away from prey that puts up any kind of resistance. Photograph © Doug Stamm/ProPhoto

The redear's native range covered an area from northern Texas to central Illinois and Indiana to South Carolina in the North, and from southern Texas to southern Florida in the South. Today, its range extends as far north as Pennsylvania and as far west as California.

The redear lives in ponds, lakes, swamps, streams, and rivers where it feeds heavily on snails. Insects, invertebrates, and small fish also make up a large part of its diet. Like the pumpkinseed, it has strong teeth in its throat that help it crush the snail's shell; this special trait earned the redear the nickname shellcracker.

SPOTTED SUNFISH

Limited to a range extending from southern Oklahoma to North Carolina in the North, and from central Texas to southern Florida in the South, the spotted sunfish, *Lepomis punctatus*, has been transplanted as widely as other sunfish. Abundant throughout the Gulf states, it has not been stocked in many waters outside its native range.

The spotted sunfish has a dark green back and is white to red-orange below, with rows of black or red-orange spots along its sides. An average spotted sunfish weighs less than ½ pound (.23 kg).

Commonly, the spotted sunfish lives in lakes, ponds, swamps, creeks, and rivers, where it feeds on insects, frogs, and toads. The fish is nicknamed the stumpknocker, because, as legend has it, the spotted sunfish runs into stumps to knock its prey into the water.

Ichthyologists recognize two subspecies of the spotted sunfish: Lepomis punctatus punctatus, *which has black spots on its sides and lives throughout much of Florida, and* Lepomis punctatus miniatus, *which does not have black spots and occupies the remainder of the spotted sunfish range. Hybrids are found in the extreme southeastern United States.* Photograph © Keith Sutton

The redbreast sunfish's closest relative is the longear sunfish. Both fish have long ear covers, but the redbreast sunfish's tends to be longer. Redbreast sunfish typically weigh ½ pound (.23 kg) or less, but under optimal growing conditions, they are capable of exceeding 2 pounds (.9 kg). An amazing 6-pound, 8-ounce (2.95 kg) specimen was reportedly caught by an ice fisherman at 11-mile Reservoir, Colorado, in 1991. Photograph © Doug Stamm/ProPhoto

REDBREAST SUNFISH

Another brightly colored sunfish species is the redbreast sunfish, *Lepomis auritus*. Its name comes from the vivid red-orange breast of the male. The fish is green on its top half and yellow with red-orange spots on its lower half. The tail and second dorsal fin are tinted red-orange. One of its distinguishing features is its long, narrow ear flap, which bears a black spot. An average redbreast weighs less than ½ pound (.23 kg), but the world record weighed-in at nearly 2 pounds (.9 kg).

The redbreast sunfish's native range included the Atlantic Coast drainages from New Brunswick to Florida. Transplantation has extended its range to the drainages of the Rio Grande and lower Mississippi River.

The redbreast is most commonly found in streams, rivers, and lakes with rocky or sandy bottoms.

BLACK CRAPPIE

Most of us do not have to travel far to find a lake or river that holds

Sunfish offer an ideal angling experience for children. They are found in large numbers and their willingness to strike a variety of prey makes them easy to catch. Many adults can trace their angling roots back to the neighborhood pond or lake where, as a child, they caught their first sunfish. Photograph © Jack Bissell

crappies, which is one reason these cooperative, great-tasting fish are among the continent's favorite panfish species. Another factor in their popularity is their tendency to congregate: Crappies live in schools that are often large and dense, making them easy to locate.

Found throughout the United States and southern Canada, the black crappie, *Pomoxis nigromaculatus*, often shares habitat with the walleye. Both prefer the cool, clear, deep water of lakes and streams. A schooling fish, black crappies hover around structure-like vegetation and submerged brush until the low-light hours of early morning and dusk, when they move as a group into open water to feed. Small fish make up a large part of their diet, along with lesser amounts of invertebrates and insects.

Crappies have disk-shaped, laterally compressed bodies, similar to those of sunfish. They are the second largest of the sunfish species, with only black bass ranking above them. Crappies have long fan-like dorsal and anal fins similar to each other in size. Two distinguishing features are an indentation above the eye and a large thin mouth. Dark green above and yellow to silver on its breast, the black crappie is recognized by the pattern of dark green marks splotched across a brassy to silver background, from head to tail. An average black crappie weighs ½ to 1 pound (.23 to .45 kg), but the fish is capable of growing to more than 5 pounds (2.3 kg). The world record caught by Lettie Robertson at Westwego Canal, Louisiana, in 1969 weighed 6 pounds (2.72 kg).

The black crappie's native range extended from southeastern Manitoba to southern Quebec in the North, and from the Gulf Coast of Texas to central Florida in the South. Through transplantation, its range has expanded dramatically to include most of the United States and southern Canada.

Spawning

When water temperatures reach the mid-60s (17°C to 19°C), black and white crappies move to their spawning grounds. In the far South, this movement may take place as early as January, while in the North, spawning may occur as late as July. Crappies select a spawning area in less than 6 feet (1.8 m) of water, over a firm bottom. The male arrives at the spawning area first, creates a dish-shaped nest by fanning his fins over the bottom, then lures a female to the nest for spawning. The female will lay as many as one hundred thousand eggs, depending on her size. The male fertilizes the eggs and remains on the nest to guard the eggs. Later he will guard the young, from predators. Females scatter from the spawning grounds to recover, suspending in deeper water near weeds or other structures.

Crappie fry feed on tiny invertebrates and grow quickly. The male soon abandons the fry to begin feeding again.

The black crappie inhabits all forty-eight of the contiguous United States as well as much of southern Canada. In many areas it shares habitat with the white crappie. When living in the same body of water, the two species of crappies compete for food, though the black crappie relies more on insects and crustaceans, while the white crappie feeds more heavily on small fish.
Photograph © Neal & MJ Mishler

White Crappie

Often confused with the black crappie, the white crappie, *Pomoxis annularis*, can be distinguished from its cousin in a number of ways. Dark green above and yellow to silver below, the white crappie's dark green markings on the sides form a series of vertical bars rather than splotchy marks. The white crappie also has six spines on its dorsal fin, while the black crappie has seven to eight. Another clue to identification is the dip over the eyes: The white crappie has a sharper, deeper dip than its cousin. A typical white crappie weighs between ½ and 1 pound (.23 and .45 kg). The world record caught by Fred L. Bright in Enid Dam, Mississippi, in 1957 weighed 5 pounds, 3 ounces (2.35 kg).

Although the two species often share habitats, the white crappie tolerates warmer, siltier water than the black crappie.

Once limited to a range stretching from eastern South Dakota to western New York in the North, and from the Gulf Coast of Texas to Alabama in the South, the white crappie now inhabits much of the United States and parts of southern Canada.

Rock Bass

Commonly spurned by anglers as a pest, the chunky, scrappy rock bass, *Ambloplites rupestris*, actually provides a better fight at the end of the line than many sunfish species. Distinguishable by its bright red eyes, the rock bass is colored green above and white to bronze below. Its sides are green and brassy with wide, dark brown vertical bars, and rows of small black spots running lengthwise along its body. It has a black spot on its ear cover, typical of many sunfish species. An average rock bass weighs between ⅓ and ½ pound (.15 and .23 kg); a large fish can reach more than 2 pounds (.9 kg). Peter Gulgin landed the world record at York River, Ontario, in 1974; it weighed-in at 3 pounds (1.36 kg).

Native to an area extending from southeastern Saskatchewan to southern Quebec in the North, and from northern Alabama to northern South Carolina in the South, the rock bass's range has expanded to include Missouri, Arkansas, Kansas, Oklahoma, and other waters west of the Mississippi.

Although it does live in lakes, the rock bass prefers well oxygenated, clear rivers and streams with rocky or sandy bottoms. There, it finds cover among weeds, rocks, or submerged brush, and feeds on insects, invertebrates, small fish, and crayfish.

Spawning

Like other sunfish species, the rock bass spawns in the spring, when water temperatures are between the high 60s and mid-70s (19°C to 25°C). The male creates a disk-shaped nest over a sand or rock bottom near

---

Both the white crappie and its closest relative, the black crappie, are among North American anglers' favorite sunfish species. Although similar in size, the white crappie tends to grow faster than the black crappie, but it does not gain girth as rapidly as its cousin. White crappies reach approximately 3 to 5 inches (7.5–13 cm) by the end of their first year and measure 7 to 8 inches (18–20 cm) by the end of their second year. Photograph © Keith Sutton

structure by fanning his fins, then attracts a female to the nest. She lays as many as ten thousand eggs, which the male then fertilizes. When the spawning ritual is complete, the male remains on the nest to guard the vulnerable eggs, and eventually the fry.

WARMOUTH

Often confused with the rock bass, the warmouth, *Lepomis gulosus*, can be distinguished from its cousin by its physical characteristics and its habitat. The warmouth has red eyes like the rock bass and similar green, brown, and bronze coloring. The warmouth however, has more mottled dark brown coloring on its sides, and lacks the rows of small black spots. It also has a series of dark brown lines running from its eye across its gill cover, a red spot alongside its black ear cover spot, and a patch of small teeth on its tongue. The warmouth also tends to be a bit larger, averaging between ½ and 1 pound (.23 and .45 kg). While the rock bass prefers cool, clear, well-oxygenated water, the warmouth more commonly inhabits quieter, warmer water in lakes, ponds, backwaters of rivers, and pools of streams. The rock bass likes a sand or gravel bottom; the warmouth tends to inhabit water with a mud bottom.

The warmouth's native range stretched from eastern Minnesota to western Pennsylvania in the North, and from New Mexico to Florida in the South. Transplantation has extended its range to a limited extent, and the warmouth currently has a range similar to that of the rock bass, including the eastern and Midwestern United States.

Spawning

Like the rock bass, the warmouth spawns in the spring when water temperatures are in the high 60s or 70s (10°C to 26°C). The male creates a disk-shaped nest by fanning his fins over the bottom. The female deposits as many as sixty thousand eggs, which the male fertilizes. After spawning, the female leaves the nesting area and the male remains behind to guard the eggs.

The warmouth, nicknamed the goggle-eye in some regions, is found in a variety of habitats, but prefers the backwaters of streams and rivers among cover such as aquatic plants, sunken trees, or stumps. Similar in appearance to the rock bass, the warmouth can be distinguished from its cousin by its blotchy brown markings and dark lines running behind each eye. Photograph © Edward G. Lines, Jr./Shedd Aquarium

The word rupestris *in the rock bass's scientific name translates to "living among rocks." The rock bass, which tolerates higher currents than most sunfish species, commonly shares habitats with the smallmouth bass in clear, cool, clean water bodies, including lakes, rivers, streams, and creeks. It chooses a habitat near rocks, logs, aquatic plants, or other submerged cover.* Photograph © Rob & Ann Simpson

Chapter 3

TROUT

*A*h, trout fishing! To be outfitted in waders and a fly vest, fighting an elegant rainbow trout in the serenity of a western, mountain stream. . . . That's the image our collective minds conjure up when we think of trout fishing. In actuality, the "classic" fly angler represents a fraction of the trout fishing opportunities in North America; the bodies of water in the United States and Canada where trout are found are as diverse as the number of trout species. One angler may travel to a tiny, farmland creek to fish for brook trout, while another may troll the deep, frigid waters of Lake Superior for lake trout. The possibilities are vast, and they would take a lifetime to explore.

Trout belong to the *Salomonidae* family, which also includes salmon, char, and whitefish. Differentiating between trout, salmon, and char is a difficult, complex, and confusing task. To simplify the job, this chapter covers mainly species with trout or char in their name.

As cold-water species, trout mainly inhabit the lakes and rivers of Canada, Alaska, and the northern, eastern, and western regions of the United States. Wherever they live, high oxygen levels, adequate cover, and hard, fairly alkaline water are important factors in sustaining healthy populations. Of course, with the diversity of waters in North America, not every lake or river in which trout live offers the perfect habitat. Bodies of water that hold ideal or near-ideal characteristics are able to maintain quality populations. Waters with marginal conditions possess trout populations teetering on a shaky ledge of survival, balanced only by the hard work of fisheries' managers and nonprofit organizations.

Rainbow trout are among the most beautiful and popular game fish in North America's freshwaters. Transplantation has established rainbow trout populations throughout much of the United States and Canada. Only southern states such as Florida and Louisiana do not have at least a few streams or reservoirs capable of sustaining rainbow trout. Photograph © Bill Buckley/The Green Agency

RAINBOW TROUT

Beautiful and easily identifiable, the rainbow trout possesses exquisite coloring, intense energy, and trophy size— all of which have helped establish it as a premier game fish. A bonanza for fisheries' managers, the rainbow trout is an easy fish to raise in hatcheries, and adaptable enough to stock in many lakes and streams outside its native range. Its now-extensive range plays a large role in the rainbow's huge popularity among anglers.

Once classified as *Salmo gairdneri*, the rainbow was reclassified in the 1980s as *Oncorhynchus mykiss* to reflect the close ties of the sea-run variety (called steelhead) to Pacific salmon. Because so many strains of rainbow trout have been mixed or diluted in hatcheries over the years, a rainbow trout's appearance can vary widely from one body of water to another. A constant is its most distinguishing feature: the red to pink stripe running lengthwise down the side of its long, powerful body. Above, the rainbow is green to blue-gray, with irregular dark spots dotting its back, sides, and fins. Below, it is white, silver, or olive. An average rainbow trout weighs 1 or 2 pounds (.45 or .9 kg), but they can grow in excess of 30 pounds (14 kg) in places such as Alaska and Canada.

The rainbow trout's native range included the West Coast of North America, from Alaska to the Baja of Mexico, and extended inland as far as Alberta and Idaho. Today, the rainbow trout is found across a majority of Canada and the northern, eastern, and western United States.

Feeding

Like most stream trout, the rainbow trout is an efficient feeder. In rivers and streams, the rainbow trout prefers faster water than the brown or brook trout. When feeding, the rainbow trout will select an area where fast water meets slow water, such as an eddy or behind a rock or submerged tree. There, it waits for food to come drifting or swimming past, pounces, then retreats to the calm waters with its prey. This feeding

The rainbow trout is easily identifiable by the pink stripe that runs along the middle of each side. The stripe's degree of intensity varies depending on the strain of rainbow trout: It is bright pink or even red in some specimens, a barely visible shadow of color in others. Bred and re-bred many times in hatcheries throughout its native range, the rainbow has taken on a wide range of appearances. Photograph © Bill Buckley/ The Green Agency

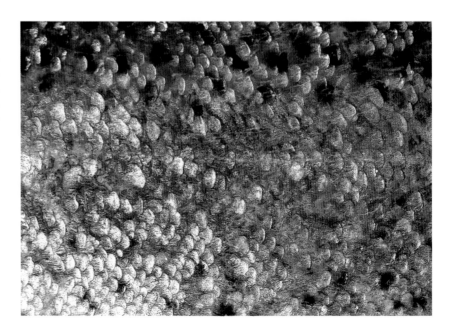

During heavy insect hatches, like this one on the Yellowstone River, trout often ignore all other food sources to focus on the hatching insect. Caddisflies, stoneflies, mayflies, and dragonflies are just a few of the common insect hatches on trout streams throughout much of North America. Photograph © Jeff Henry/Roche Jaune Pictures, Inc.

method conserves energy that would be wasted if the rainbow trout swam around in fast water in search of food.

In lakes, where the rainbow trout does not have to deal with current, it has more freedom to move around and search for food. One day it may feed on the surface near shore, and the next day it may feed 20 feet (5 m) below the surface, in the middle of the lake.

Aquatic insects are the staple of the average rainbow trout's diet, but it also feeds on terrestrial insects, fish, worms, and crayfish. During insect hatches, a small rainbow trout may key in on the hatch and ignore all other food. A 5- to 10-pound (2.3- to 4.5-kilogram) rainbow trout is more likely to nab a small fish for a meal.

Spawning

The rainbow trout, which reaches sexual maturity at age three or four, is one of the few trout species to spawn in the spring—anytime between late winter and early summer. The female arrives at the spawning area first and uses her tail and fin to dig a redd, or nest. She usually selects an area in riffles or at the back of a pool, commonly over gravel. She then lays her eggs, which may number as many as six thousand, depending on her size. The male moves over the nest, close to the female, and fertilizes the eggs.

The rainbow trout's eggs lodge in the gravel and incubate for a month to six weeks before hatching. Once hatched, rainbow trout fry grow quickly and soon are able to feed on aquatic insects. Although the fertilization rate of rainbow trout eggs can exceed 90 percent, the rate of survival among the fry is sometimes less than 1 percent. This high mortality rate results from predation from fish and birds, and natural disasters such as flash flooding or drought.

BROOK TROUT

Nature's elegant paintbrush created a masterpiece when it ornamented the stunning brook trout, *Salvelinus fontinalis*. Brilliant spots of pink, red, or purple, haloed in blue, adorn green to black sides. Wavy, wormlike lines of green or cream work their way across the back from head to tail. Breeding males develop a fiery red lower side that screams out in a rage of beauty.

This beautiful fish, despite its name, is actually a char. Averaging ½ to 1 pound (.23 to .45 kg) in streams, and 2 to 3 pounds (.9 to 1.4 kg) in some lakes and along the Atlantic Coast, the growth potential of a brook trout depends greatly on its habitat. In a small overcrowded brook, a five-year-old brook trout (or brookie as it is commonly called) may weigh ½ pound (.23 kg), while a three-year-old may grow to 3 pounds (1.4 kg) in a healthy lake. Wherever it lives, the brook trout rarely grows to more

A rainbow trout dances across the surface of the water while it battles to shake free from a hook. Although they are not among the largest, pound-for-pound rainbow trout can match nearly any other game fish on the continent in fighting ability. Tough, aggressive, and powerful when hooked, rainbows put up an excellent fight against any angler. Photograph © Doug Stamm/ ProPhoto

than 5 pounds (2.3 kg) and seldom lives longer than five years. The world record brookie, caught by Dr. W. J. Cook at the Nipigon River in Ontario in 1916, weighed an astounding 14 pounds, 8 ounces (6.58 kg).

The native range of the brook trout stretched from eastern Manitoba to Labrador in the North, and from eastern Minnesota to New Jersey, down through the Appalachian Mountains to Georgia in the South. Later, it was introduced to much of the Rocky Mountain region, from British Columbia to Nevada and Utah.

Habitat

Unlike the rainbow trout, which adapts well to a variety of conditions, the brook trout is particular about its habitat. The brookie needs cold, clear, well-oxygenated water. Its peak activity occurs when water temperatures range in the mid- to high 50s (12°C to 15°C). When temperatures rise to the mid- to high 60s (17°C to 21°C), a brook trout will usually leave in search of cooler water. Changes in the environment can reduce or totally eradicate brook trout populations, which cannot tolerate the heated, dirty water brought about by development and pollution.

Although the brook trout demands specific habitat conditions, it lives in a wide spectrum of waters, from tiny gurgling brooks an angler could step across, to Lake Superior, the world's largest lake.

Wherever it lives, the brook trout's diet consists primarily of aquatic insects, along with terrestrial insects, small fish, crayfish, and frogs.

Spawning

Depending on latitude and weather, the brook trout spawn usually occurs between the months of October and December. Spawning sites are chosen in gravelly riffles, where flowing water oxygenates eggs and keeps them free from silt. The female moves into the spawning area first and creates a shallow redd by fanning and digging with her tail. When an

The brook trout needs a more specific environment than brown, rainbow, and other trout. Brookies require cold, clean water and high oxygen levels. Because of their sensitivity to environmental conditions, when brook trout disappear from a water body, it is usually the first sign of adverse changes to the ecosystem. Brook trout were eradicated from numerous streams in the eastern United States by pollution and development. Photograph © Jim Yuskavitch

Brook trout are not really trout, but a species of char. Although much smaller than char species like the lake trout and Arctic char, brook trout are extremely popular with anglers because of their beauty and willingness to strike a variety of prey. In their breeding colors, male brook trout are arguably the most gorgeous freshwater fish in North America. Photograph © Mark Giovanetti/ProPhoto

Wherever trout live in North America it is likely a fly angler will be nearby. The artificial flies they use for bait represent the a trout's natural food items, including aquatic insects, terrestrial insects, and minnows. At times, insects represent more than 90 percent of a trout's diet, but other creatures such as tadpoles, leeches, worms, and crayfish are common meals. Photograph © Alan and Sandy Carey

The splake is a hatchery-born, artificial hybrid of a lake trout and brook trout. It began gaining popularity with Great Lakes anglers during the 1950s, after sea lampreys decimated lake trout populations. Today, splake are found throughout much of the northern United States and Canada from the Sierra Nevadas to New England. Photograph © Bill Vaznis/The Green Agency

eager male is ready, she lays her eggs, which number in the hundreds or thousands depending on her size. The male, who develops a hooked jaw during the spawn and may have battled other males for the right to spawn with this female, rushes in to fertilize the eggs as soon as they are released. When the spawning act is complete, the female covers the eggs with gravel by digging out another nest. She spawns again in the new redd, and may spawn several times before she is finished.

The eggs remain on the stream bed until they hatch in late winter or spring. At first, the young brookies feed on their yolk sacs, then soon move to the surface to feed on microscopic organisms. By summer, the fry reach nearly 2 inches (5 cm) in length and are able to feed on larger aquatic insects.

In lakes, brook trout will congregate at the mouth of a tributary, then move up the river or stream to spawn. Anadromous brook trout, like those found off the northeastern Atlantic Coast and in Lake Superior, follow a similar pattern.

SPLAKE

A hatchery hybrid, the splake is a cross between a male brook trout and a female lake trout. Fisheries' managers have found the splake suitable for many cold water lakes in Canada and the northern United States. The hybrid grows faster than a lake trout and larger than a brook trout, occasionally exceeding ten pounds. Although similar in appearance to the brook trout, the splake's colors tend to be more drab.

BROWN TROUT

Among the immigrants traveling from Europe to America in the 1880s were the ancestors of the North American brown trout, *Salmo trutta*. Brought to the United States from Germany and Scotland in 1883 and 1885, the brown trout has grown to become a classic North American game fish. Its adaptability to a variety of habitat conditions, combined with its beauty, size, and abundance, helped the brown trout carve out a place as one of the continent's most popular game fish.

Throughout its range, the brown trout inhabits cool, well-oxygenated streams and cold lakes. Compared to most trout species, though, the brown trout possesses a remarkable tolerance for warm water. Its ideal temperature range is between the mid-50s and high 60s (12°C to 21°C)—about ten degrees Fahrenheit (six degrees Celsius) higher than an average rainbow or brook trout can handle. This tolerance is a blessing for North American trout anglers, who can now fish for trout in Southern states, where trout previously could not survive. Stockings of brown trout have also flourished in streams where changing conditions created a habitat intolerable for native brook trout. First stocked in Michigan and New York, the brown trout's range has steadily expanded to include most of North America's cold-water fisheries.

Named in a plain and understated way for its primary color, the brown trout truly is a magnificent species to behold. Colored dark brown to olive above, fading to light brown or golden yellow down its sides, the brown trout is freckled across its head, back and sides with black and red spots haloed in cream or white. Though it is capable of exceeding 30 pounds (14 kg) in some waters, the average brown trout weighs between ½ pound and 2 pounds (.23 and .9 kg).

The brown trout's main food source is aquatic insects, as any fly fisherman can attest, but terrestrial insects, worms, small fish, and crayfish are also important parts of its diet.

Spawning

Brown trout are fall spawners. Eggs usually are laid in the riffle areas of the main stream, but brown trout also may move into smaller tributaries to spawn. The female uses her tail to dig out two, three, or even four redds, then lays as many as six thousand eggs in her nests. A waiting male moves in quickly to fertilize the eggs at each redd. It may take two or three males to fertilize all the eggs laid by a single female.

Anadromous brown trout, which are more silvery in color, are found in the Atlantic Ocean and the Great Lakes where they spend most of their life, migrating into tributaries only to spawn.

Brown trout eggs hatch in the late winter, and the fry spend their earliest days feeding on microscopic organisms near the bottom of the stream. As the fish grow, they will begin to take food from the surface. Young anadromous brown trout spend up to three years in the tributary before moving out to the lake or ocean.

Brown trout are one of the most popular North American freshwater game fish among fly fishermen and women. They are also one of the few game fish species on the continent that is not indigenous to North America. Brown trout arrived from Europe in the late nineteenth century and were introduced to large sections of the United States and Canada. Today, North American anglers can fish for brown trout in nearly every state and most provinces. Photograph © Bill Buckley/ The Green Agency

Small- to medium-sized brown trout feed mainly on aquatic insects, and their active feeding periods can turn on and off with hatches of various insects, ending just as quickly as they begin. This feeding phenomena can drive unprepared or inexperienced anglers crazy. In contrast, large brown trout are more likely to feed on prey suited to their size, such as small fish, leeches, and crayfish. Photograph © Bill Buckley/The Green Agency

The lake trout is the largest member of North America's char family. Capable of growing in excess of 100 pounds (45 kg), lake trout are most commonly found in cold, deep water. Although the lake trout's native range extended no further south than the Great Lakes, transplantation has opened lake trout fishing opportunities in reservoirs and mountain lakes in southwestern states such as New Mexico, California, Nevada, and Utah. Limited stocking also has occurred in south-central states such as Arkansas, Kentucky, and Tennessee. Photograph © Bill Vaznis/The Green Agency

LAKE TROUT

Along the shores of the Great Lakes, tales abound of commercial fishing nets drawing in lake trout weighing over 100 pounds (45 kg). Although no sport angler has ever landed such a catch, the lake trout, *Salvelinus namaycush*, is the largest North American trout and has made for some epic catches, such as the world record caught by Lloyd E. Bull in 1995 at Great Bear Lake, Northwest Territory, which weighed 72 pounds, 4 ounces (32.77 kg).

The lake trout, also known as the Mackinaw in some regions, belongs to the char family and is closely related to the brook trout. Its dark green to gray body is dotted with cream or yellow spots. It has a white belly and a deeply forked tail. An average lake trout, or laker, weighs between 3 and 8 pounds (1.4 and 3.6 kg), depending on the region it inhabits, but lake trout weighing more than 20 pounds (9 kg) are by no means uncommon.

The lake trout is native to an area stretching from the Arctic reaches of Alaska to Labrador in the North, and from Montana to New York in the South. Successful introductions extended its range to mountainous lakes in Idaho, Wyoming, Colorado, Utah, Oregon, New Mexico, Nevada, and California.

Habitat

The lake trout inhabits cold water, often at depths of 100 feet (30 m) or more. In some areas, the lake trout survives in small, shallower lakes or in lake-like rivers, but wherever it lives, it requires cold, clear, well-oxygenated water. The lake trout prefers temperatures around 40°F (4°C), tolerates water in the 50s (10°C to 15°C), and seeks new water when temperatures rise to the low 60s (16°C to 17°C). Lake trout that inhabit huge bodies of water such as the Great Lakes, are usually able to find optimal water temperatures even during the heat of summer.

Most of a lake trout's time is spent near the lake's bottom, where it feeds heavily on small fish like the alewife, smelt, ciscoes, suckers, yellow perch, and whitefish. It occasionally moves into shallower water to feed in the early morning or evening, and in spring after ice-out. The laker tends to come up near the surface in the spring and fall, and in some very cold lakes in the far North, it may stay near the surface much of the summer.

Spawning

Like most trout species, the lake trout spawns in the fall. Usually spawning occurs just before the water ices up —as early as August in the far northern regions of its range and as late as December in the southern regions.

Lake trout commonly spawn in deep water over gravel or a reef. Sometimes, lakers will move to the mouth of a tributary, or even into the lower sections of a tributary, to spawn. The males, which reach sexual maturity around age five, arrive at the spawning area first; the females, which may take as long as nine years to reach sexual maturity, follow a few days later. Lake trout do not build a nest for the eggs; instead, the female deposits between two thousand and seventeen thousand eggs on the bottom, and the male fertilizes the eggs as they fall into protective spaces between the gravel.

The eggs hatch in two to five months. The newly hatched fry move quickly out to the safety of deep water, where the chances of other fish preying on them are significantly reduced.

CUTTHROAT TROUT

Named for the bright red gashes of coloring on its lower jaw, the cutthroat trout, *Oncorhynchus clarki*, varies dramatically in appearance from one region to another. The cutthroat's body color ranges from green-yellow in some regions on the continent, to red in others, to blue-green in others, and a combination of these colors in still other regions. This remarkable color variance is due to the dozens of subspecies—some of which are common, while others are endangered or extinct. All cutthroats, though, have the crimson marking on the jaw and many black spots dotted across the body. While an average freshwater cutthroat weighs 1 to 2 pounds, the larger silver-colored sea-run cutthroat averages 2 to 4 pounds (.9 to 1.8 kg).

The cutthroat is a western trout. Its native range included the Pacific Coast from Alaska to northern California, and the Rocky Mountains from British Columbia and Alberta to Arizona and New Mexico. Transplantation has expanded its range to numerous waters outside its native range.

Like most trout species, the cutthroat prefers a habitat of cold, clear, well-oxygenated water and is at home in small streams, large rivers, or lakes. The Pacific Coast strain of cutthroats spend most of their time in the ocean, returning to the rivers in which they were born only to spawn.

Spawning

The time at which the cutthroat spawns varies drastically from region to region. In some waters, it may spawn in late winter, while in another area the cutthroat may spawn in late summer. The cutthroat selects a spawning ground in fast, shallow water, where eggs receive plenty of oxygen and remain silt free. Cutthroats that live in lakes must move into a tributary to find these ideal conditions.

The female builds one or more nests by digging out the gravel with her tail. She deposits hundreds to thousands of eggs, depending on her size, and the male fertilizes them. When the spawning act is complete, the female covers the eggs to protect them and keep them in place. The majority of cutthroats spawn just once in a lifetime, but a few may reproduce as many as three to four times.

In about two months the eggs hatch. The fry will begin feeding on tiny zooplankton before graduating to insects. The young of sea-run or lake-dwelling cutthroats spend their first two years in the river, then migrate to the sea or lake.

Inland cutthroat trout mainly feed on aquatic and terrestrial insects, but their diet also includes sculpins and other fish, crayfish, frogs, salamanders, and fish eggs. Similarly, sea-run cutthroats feed primarily on aquatic insects, but have been known to eat juvenile coho salmon. Photograph © Robert E. Barber

The cutthroat trout is aptly named for the blood-colored strips found on each side of its jaw. These gashes of color are usually bright on inland fish, dull or absent on sea-run varieties. The cutthroat is closely related to the rainbow trout and often interbreeds with its cousin. Photograph © Bill Buckley/The Green Agency

During the spawning run, the male Arctic char's back turns blue and its belly turns red to orange in a beautiful display of breeding color. In some land-locked areas, males hold these colors throughout the year. Typically though, the brilliant colors fade dramatically during the non-spawning months, and, in some cases, the fish even appear sil-very throughout. Photograph © Ken Marsh

ARCTIC CHAR

Found mainly in the northernmost reaches of North America, the Arc-tic char, *Salvelinus alpinus*, is a species that can live in very cold water. No other game fish on the continent lives as far north as the Arctic char. Its native range extended from western Alaska through the Arctic drain-ages of the Northwest Territory, to the Hudson Bay drainages of Ontario and Quebec, to the Atlantic drainages of Labrador and Newfoundland.

Sea-run Arctic char are green to brown above, with red to pink spots on their sides, while landlocked varieties tend to be more silvery, with some males taking on the breeding colors—dark blue to green above, with bright red bellies—year round. The average Arctic char weighs from 3 to 5 pounds (1.4 to 2.3 kg), but can grow in excess of 25 pounds (11 kg). The world record caught by Jeffery Lee Ward at the Tree River in the Northwest Territory in 1981 weighed 32 pounds, 9 ounces (14.77 kg).

The Arctic char feeds on small fish, crustaceans, and shrimp, with fish comprising the majority of its diet.

Spawning

Because of its extreme northern range, the Arctic char spawns in early autumn, when tributaries flow without ice and migration upstream is possible. For fish that migrate hundreds of miles to reach the spawning grounds, the trip up the tributaries begins as early as July.

The female Arctic char, unlike most of its cousins, does not make a nest. She simply deposits her eggs over gravel in an area with adequate flow, and the male fertilizes them. An adult Arctic char usually returns to its lake right away in the fall, though a sea-run Arctic char usually stays in the river until spring.

The eggs remain on the bottom until spring, when the fry hatch into an ice-cold world. The sea-run fry spend their first year of life in the river, then move out to sea.

DOLLY VARDEN

Belonging to the char family, the Dolly Varden, *Salvelinus malma*, lives in cold-water lakes and rivers west of the Rocky Mountains. Its native range included Alaska, western British Columbia, Puget Sound, Washington, and McCloud River, California. It is common still today throughout much of its range, with the exception of the McCloud River drainage.

Most young anadromous Dolly Varden leave the river of their birth by their second year to move out to sea, but in rare cases stay inland for up to six years. Dolly Varden are capable of spawning more than once in their lifetime, with females more likely to be multiple spawners than males. Males commonly die after spawning due to injuries received fighting other males during the spawning run. Photograph © Ken Marsh

Named for the cherry-colored dress of the heroine in Charles Dickens' novel *Barnaby Rudge*, the Dolly Varden is a colorful fish whose markings vary from one area to the next. In freshwater, the Dolly Varden is green to brown above and yellow-white below, with yellow, red, or orange spots on the sides, while anadromous Dolly Vardens are blue above and silvery on the sides, with paler colored spots. In the fall or early winter, spawning males develop a bright orange belly, similar to that of the brook trout, females' bellies turn a paler orange. On average, the Dolly Varden weighs 3 to 5 pounds (1.4 to 2.3 kg), though it can grow to more than 20 pounds (9 kg).

Although it plays an important role as a game fish in the West, the Dolly Varden has long been despised by commercial salmon netters and some sport anglers because it is a major predator of young salmon.

Spawning

Like other char, the Dolly Varden spawns in the fall or early winter. Sea-run parents seek a spawning ground in shallow water with a gravel bottom, while lake-dwelling fish choose a tributary stream or spawn on the lake bottom. The fry hatch in spring and remain in the river for up to two years before making the journey to the sea or lake.

BULL TROUT

Once thought to be a subspecies of Dolly Varden, the bull trout, *Salvelinus confluentus*, is now recognized as a separate species. Although its appearance is nearly a mirror image of the Dolly Varden, a few subtle differences exist between the two species. For instance, the bull trout has a longer, fatter head and its eyes are higher on its head. The most reliable way to differentiate between the two is to check the pores under the fish's jaw: The bull trout has seven to nine mandible pores, while the Dolly Varden has six.

Ranges overlap in some areas, but the bull trout lives more often in cold, inland mountain streams and lakes and rarely retreats to the sea like the anadromous Dolly Varden. The bull trout's range includes an area extending from the southern Yukon, through central British Columbia and Alberta, into Montana, Idaho, Washington, Oregon, and northern California.

GOLDEN TROUT

Like a small, beautiful gem lying in a rugged mountain stream or western lake, the golden trout, *Oncorhynchus aguabonita*, is highly sought after by anglers, yet almost wholly inaccessible. Native only to the Kern River basin in California, at elevations of 8,000 feet (2,400 m) or higher, the golden trout was introduced to hundreds of high-elevation lakes and streams in the mountain states of the West. Most waters it inhabits are remote and accessible only by horseback or on foot.

The intense coloring of the golden trout is what most often sends anglers out in search of this beautiful species. Its olive green back, speckled with black spots, descends into brilliant red bars on the sides. Its

Factors such as dam construction, logging, and overfishing have severely reduced the bull trout's populations and led to its listing as a threatened species. Also, the introduction of nonnative trout, such as the brook trout, has contributed to the bull trout's decline. Bull and brook trout often spawn with each other, resulting in an infertile hybrid. More than one-half of the bull trout's remaining populations inhabit the waters of Montana. Photograph © Jim Yuskavitch

The golden trout is admired by anglers for its beauty more than its size. Many anglers trek miles across high-elevation trails on horseback or on foot to reach the remote lakes that hold golden trout. Although native to only a small part of the Sierra Nevada Mountains, the golden trout was transplanted to numerous lakes throughout the Rocky Mountains. Photograph © Ron Sanford

golden lower side gives way to a bright red belly. Golden trout usually do not grow very large, often weighing less than 1 pound (.45 kg) and growing less than 12 inches (30 cm) in length. In some lakes however, they can reach trophy size, such as the world record caught by Chas S. Reed in Cook's Lake, Wyoming, in 1948, that weighed 11 pounds (4.99 kg).

The golden trout, which spawns in late spring to early summer, usually selects a spawning area in a river or stream with substantial flow over gravel; golden trout that live in lakes without tributary streams are forced to spawn in shallow water. The spawning migration is short; once there, the female creates a nest and deposits her eggs, which the male quickly fertilizes. After hatching, the fry feed on tiny zooplankton and crustaceans. The fry of lake-run fish spend up to one year in the stream before moving to the lake.

APACHE TROUT

Protected as a threatened species, the Apache trout, *Oncorhynchus apache*, is one of North America's rarest trout species. Native only to the Upper Salt and Little Colorado river systems of Arizona, the Apache's numbers were devastated by competition from other trout species and hybridization with the rainbow trout. Management efforts are slowly restoring the Apache to parts of its range.

The Apache is bright yellow with black spots across its body. It lives in cold, high-elevation streams and lakes. In streams, Apache trout rarely exceed 1 pound (.45 kg), while lake-dwelling fish can grow to more than 2 pounds (.9 kg). An Apache weighing over 5 pounds (2.3 kg) is a rare catch.

The Apache trout was named Arizona's state fish in 1986 in order to raise awareness of its severely declining population. Competition from nonnative rainbow and other trout, as well as hybridization with the rainbow, led to the Apache trout's disappearance in 95 percent of its native waters. Among the efforts to restore Apache trout populations was the construction of a special hatchery by the White Mountain Apache Tribe, which is dedicated to protecting the fish and re-establishing it in native waters. Photograph © Jim Yuskavitch

Approximately one month after the spring spawn, Arctic grayling move to their summer feeding areas, which can range from a few miles to more than 75 miles (120 km) away. At the feeding grounds, the grayling segregate by age, with the oldest fish staking out the upstream areas, the subadults in the middle reaches, and the juveniles downstream. Photograph © Edward G. Lines, Jr./Shedd Aquarium

ARCTIC GRAYLING

Although it inhabits many of the same waters as trout and salmon, the Arctic grayling, *Thymallus arcticus*, is only a distant relative of these species. Like its cousins, it prefers a habitat of cold, clear rivers and lakes in the northern reaches of the continent. Its native range stretched from northern Alaska to central Northwest Territory in the North, and from western British Columbia to northern Manitoba in the South. It was native also to sections of Michigan and western Montana. Today, anglers in the United States fish for grayling through much of the Rocky Mountain region, thanks to successful transplantation.

Although its general body shape is similar to a trout's, the Arctic grayling, with its distinctive, fan-like dorsal fin, cannot be mistaken for any other species. Its body is dark blue to gray above, and blue to silver below, with a few dark spots on its sides. The distinguishing dorsal fin is larger on males than females and dotted with rows of red to green spots. Grayling average about 1 pound (.45 kg), though the world record caught by Jeanne P. Branson at Katseyedie River, Northwest Territory, in 1967 weighed 5 pounds, 15 ounces (2.69 kg).

~ Mottled Sculpin ~

The mottled sculpin, Cottus bairdi, is an important food source for lake trout and large brook and brown trout in the cold-water lakes and streams of the Great Lakes region, Hudson Bay drainages, and Rocky Mountain states. Like the trout, it lives in a range of areas, stretching from Manitoba to northern Quebec in the North, from Missouri to South Carolina in the South, and the Rocky Mountain states from Washington to Colorado.

A small, scaleless fish averaging about 4 inches (10 cm) in length, the mottled sculpin has a thick head that tapers down to a thin tail. It has a brown back, a white underside, and dark brown to black mottling on the back and sides. Its large, fan-like pectoral fins have brown bands, as do its dorsal fin, anal fin, and tail.

An estimated twenty-six species of sculpins inhabit North America's freshwaters. They commonly live amongst rocks and stones at the bottom of rivers, streams, and lakes.

The mottled sculpin shares an important predator/prey relationship with most of North America's trout and char because it inhabits many of the continent's clear, cold streams and lakes. The mottled sculpin's preferred habitat includes the riffles and runs of creeks, areas where springs enter a stream, and lakes with rocky shallows. Photograph © Michael Quinton

Spawning

Grayling spawn in the spring, usually following ice-out. In rivers, they move upstream or into smaller tributaries to spawn. In lakes, they migrate into a tributary stream or, if no streams are available, into shallow water. The female does not dig out a nest; instead, she deposits her one thousand to five thousand adhesive eggs over gravel. The male, who stays close to her during the spawning act, fertilizes the eggs simultaneously.

Two to three weeks after fertilization, the grayling eggs hatch. In the first days of life the fry feed on their yolk sacs, then soon begin feeding on tiny plankton. As they grow, the young grayling graduate to larger food items like aquatic insects. An adult grayling feeds on a variety of aquatic and terrestrial insects, making it a natural target for fly anglers.

SALMON

*T*he life of a salmon is a tragic struggle in which, each year, life and death intertwine for one bittersweet moment. It is a story of determination that sees the heroes fall, but from their demise rises a new hope for the future. The salmon's life story differs greatly from that of most North American freshwater game fish, for in the lives of most salmon species, the succession of the species is dependent on the death of a whole generation. From the first moment an egg is deposited on the river bottom until the salmon's final, fatal journey years later, its life is a series of steps, preparing it for a one-way, no-turning-back migration, which ends in the passing of one generation and beginning of a new one.

Young salmon, called parr, spend the first one to three years of life in the river, where they must avoid predation, floods, drought, and other obstacles, while feeding and growing in preparation for their first significant move. When development in freshwater is complete, the salmon, now graduated from parr to smolt, move out to the vast waters of the sea or lake, where they feed heavily on fish and insects. A salmon in the sea grows quickly, gaining the strength it will need for its final journey, all the while facing an endless threat from a variety of predators. In its last year, it begins a migration back to the river from which it came, called back by an inner alarm clock to perform its final task.

Just before the spawn, the salmon stage at the river mouth, waiting anxiously for water levels to rise and temperatures to reach the ideal range. Often, hundreds or thousands of salmon can be seen offshore, rolling and porpoising at the surface in preparation for their migration.

~⊱⊰~

The chinook or king salmon is the largest of the Pacific salmon species. Monsters like this 40-pounder (18-kg) caught in Alaska are not uncommon in Pacific waters, while Great Lakes chinooks rarely reach such a size. Like this one, chinooks are silvery throughout prior to their spawning migration, but their appearance changes dramatically during their run upstream. Photograph © William H. Mullins

When the time is right, the salmon begin the trip upstream. At first, only a handful of salmon enter the river, but as conditions near the optimal point, droves of salmon explode into the river, battling their way upstream in a desperate frenzy. Depending on the river, the salmon may travel 1 mile (1.6 km) or hundreds of miles to reach the spawning grounds, fighting strong currents, rapids, and waterfalls along the way.

As they move upstream, the fish undergo physical changes. Their silvery color darkens. Their digestive system shrinks to make room for expanding reproductive organs, and feeding ceases. The male changes most dramatically, developing an angry, hooked jaw called a kype, and in some cases, a humped back.

As they near the spawning grounds, the salmon use their sense of smell to find the place where their lives began years before. When the site is located, the female uses her body to dig out a nest in the gravel bottom. She lays her eggs, then the male moves in to fertilize them. After his milt is released, the female moves in again, using her last bits of energy to cover the eggs with gravel. With their task complete, the exhausted salmon deteriorate quickly and soon die.

Not all salmon species perish after spawning, but most do. The steelhead and Atlantic salmon for example, may survive and return to spawn several times. For the chinook, coho, and sockeye salmon, however, spawning is fatal.

Salmon belong to the *Oncorhynchus* genus of the *Salmonidae* family, which also includes the cutthroat and golden trout. They are native to the northern Pacific and Atlantic Coasts; successful transplantation has expanded some species' ranges to inland waters— most notably the Great Lakes.

CHINOOK SALMON

Massive, powerful, and beautiful, the chinook or king salmon, *Oncorhynchus tshawytscha*, is arguably the most impressive game fish in North America's freshwaters. Not only is it the largest salmon species, but it is also one of the most enormous game fish on the continent. In most areas an average adult chinook weighs a respectable 20 to 25 pounds (9 to 11 kg), and in some parts of its range, a 50- or 60-pound (22.5- or 27-kg) chinook is not uncommon. The world record weighed nearly 100 pounds (45 kg); commercial netters have harvested even larger chinooks.

Living at sea or in a lake, the chinook is a stunning fish. Its body is silvery with a green, gray or blue back, and black spots on its back, upper fins, and tail. A large male may take on a dull reddish color on its sides. An angler can differentiate a chinook from other Pacific salmon by the fish's dark gums, which set it apart from its cousins.

During the spawning run, chinooks lose much of their beauty. Most noticeably, their colors darken and turn greenish-brown to purple. By the time chinooks reach the spawning grounds, their bodies are often cut and bruised, with flesh hanging loose from their belly or sides. For anyone who sees this transformation, it is no surprise the fish perish

Adult chinook salmon move upstream during the final journey of their lives. Chinooks can travel incredible distances some-times up to 1,000 miles (1,600 km) to reach their spawning grounds. In some areas, chinooks will clear waterfalls, whitewater rapids, and other natural hurdles along the way. The fish move upstream with one purpose: To continue the life cycle of the species. Photograph © Michael Quinton

after spawning. Death though, is not directly related to exhaustion from the spawning run, but rather to physiological changes, that occur during the spawning migration.

Chinooks typically spawn in the fall, and their offspring hatch in the spring, though this timetable varies between locations. The parr spend less than a year in the river before migrating to the sea or lake as smolts.

Although the chinook is commonly considered a four year salmon (meaning it typically lives four years), some live as long as eight years. Those chinooks that survive beyond the normal life span usually, as one might imagine, attain much larger sizes than their younger siblings.

The chinook's native range stretched from the Arctic drainages of northwestern Alaska, south along the Pacific Coast to California. During the spawning runs, some chinooks travel hundreds of miles, or in some cases, more than 1,000 miles (1,600 km) across Alaska, the Northwest Territory, British Columbia, Washington, Oregon, and even into Idaho. Stocking has expanded the chinook's range to a few inland waters. The most successful introduction was to the Great Lakes, where the chinook has fared well since its first transplantation in 1967. Ironically, the chinook is flourishing in nonnative lakes like Erie, Michigan, and Superior, but through much of its native range, the salmon is in trouble. Pressure from commercial netters and sport anglers, environmental deterioration, and dam construction have sent its populations spiraling downward.

Weeks or even months after beginning its upstream migration, the chinook salmon completes the spawning act, quickly deteriorates, and dies. The dark, hideous mask of its death bears little resemblance to the powerful, silvery salmon that started the upstream journey. Following the spawn, the spawning grounds turn into a graveyard of rotting salmon, which become food for a variety of birds and animals.
Photograph © Michael Quinton

COHO SALMON

Although not as large as the chinook, the coho or silver salmon, *Oncorhynchus kisutch*, is one of the most highly prized Pacific salmon species. Treasured by anglers for its exquisite taste and back-breaking power, the coho hits bait hard, and pound-for-pound provides one of the best fights of any North American freshwater game fish.

In the sea or lake, the coho's coloring is silver, with a dark blue back

The coho or silver salmon is one of the most popular Pacific salmon species among sport anglers. Known for its power and strength, cohos are considered one of the hardest-fighting fish in North America. Anglers also value cohos for their delectable meat, which many claim to be the best tasting among Pacific salmon. Photograph © Marion Allen Stirrup

and black spots running along its back and upper tail. While on its spawning run, the coho's head, back, and fins turn green. The male's lower sides become a brilliant red, while the female's change to a faded red or pink. An average adult coho weighs between 5 and 10 pounds (2.3 to 4.5 kg), but cohos weighing more than 15 pounds (6.8 kg) are not unheard of.

Considered a three-year salmon, some cohos survive a year or two beyond their target age. Whether it lives three or four years, the coho's life ends with the completion of it spawning migration.

The coho migrates into large and small rivers, usually not traveling as far as the chinook to reach its spawning grounds. During the spawn, the male commonly displays vicious behavior, battling other males with its hooked jaw for the right to spawn with a female.

The coho spawns in fall or early winter. Once fertilized, the eggs incubate for one to two months before hatching. The parr spend about one to two years in the river before migrating to the sea or lake as smolts.

The coho's native range included an area extending from the Arctic drainages of northern Alaska, south to central California. Introductions to the Great Lakes, Lake Champlain, and parts of New England have produced new fisheries outside its native range, with varying levels of success.

Steelhead are one of the most prized game fish along the Pacific coast and in the Great Lakes. Anglers value steelhead for their beauty, power, and size. Unfortunately, dams, logging, and pollution have taken a toll on steelhead populations along the Pacific coast. Human construction and habitat destruction have drastically reduced the quality of steelhead angling in many rivers and eliminated populations in others. Photograph © Mark Giovanetti/ProPhoto

STEELHEAD

Although the steelhead, *Oncorhynchus mykiss*, is closely related to Pacific salmon and commonly grouped with them, it is actually a sea-run variety of rainbow trout. Despite this classification, most anglers draw a distinct difference between anadromous steelhead and land-locked rainbow trout.

Like silent chrome missiles on a guided course, steelhead truly are beautiful specimens to behold when migrating upstream on their annual spawning run. Their elegance and strength draw countless anglers to the tributaries of the Pacific coast and Great Lakes to do battle with these magnificent fish.

Native to the Pacific Coast from Alaska to California, the steelhead was successfully introduced to the Great Lakes in 1895. Over a century later, populations thrive in each of the Great Lakes.

Unlike most salmon species, the steelhead can survive the arduous spawning migration. The fish spends up to the first three years of its life in the river, then moves out to the sea or lake to live, returning to the river to spawn about three years later. A steelhead is capable of spawning three or four times in its life.

The steelhead is a spring spawner. After breeding, some adults move quickly back to the sea or lake, while others remain in the river for more than a week. Steelhead eggs incubate on the gravel bottom as brief as three weeks and up to three months, depending on river conditions.

While living in the sea or in a lake, the steelhead is chrome colored, but as it moves upstream on its spawning run, the fish takes on the pinkish stripe of the rainbow trout. Throughout much of its range, the steelhead averages about 10 pounds (4.5 kg); in parts of the Pacific Coast, however, steelhead commonly reach 25 to 30 pounds (11.3 to 14 kg).

Young steelhead have a low chance of reaching adulthood. High numbers of fry die in the river due to predation, floods, or drought and never begin the journey to the sea. It is estimated that fewer than 10 percent of steelhead smolt that survive the trip to the sea will ever return to spawn. Photograph © Bill Vaznis/The Green Agency

ATLANTIC SALMON

For over a century, New Englanders and eastern Canadian anglers have devoutly fished the migratory run of the Atlantic salmon, *Salmo salar*. This time-honored tradition has made the Atlantic salmon, nearly peerless with its loyal and long-standing following, one of the most important game fish species of the northern Atlantic Coast.

More closely related to anadromous trout, such as the brook or brown, than to other species named "salmon," the Atlantic salmon can, and often does, survive the spawning run. It spends its first one to three years in the river where it was born before moving out to sea, where the fish grows for two or more years before returning to its native river to spawn. Atlantic salmon spawn in late summer to fall, though they sometimes enter tributaries as early as June. Some fish do die after spawning, but many return to the lake or sea. The Atlantic may spawn three or four times during its life, with females being more likely to repeatedly spawn than males.

At sea, the Atlantic has silvery sides and a brownish-green to blue back, with black spots, or "x" marks, on its head, sides, and back. In freshwater, the fish turns brassy or brown. An average North American Atlantic weighs about 10 pounds (4.5 kg), depending on where it lives, yet anglers occasionally catch Atlantics weighing more than 20 pounds (9 kg).

In North America, the Atlantic's native range stretched from northeastern Quebec, south along the Atlantic Coast to Connecticut, and inland as far as Lake Ontario. Landlocked Atlantics are native to lakes in Maine and eastern Canada. Today, the Atlantic has disappeared from parts of its native range, sadly being killed off by pollution and development. Environmental efforts have succeeded in restoring some of its lost habitat, but not all. Attempts to introduce the Atlantic to inland waters like the Great Lakes have not fared well, paling next to the success of chinook salmon and steelhead transplantations. In the past, fisheries' managers in Canada, Minnesota, Wisconsin, and Michigan have attempted to stock the Atlantic salmon in the Great Lakes; today, only Michigan continues its Atlantic salmon stocking program.

Although limited numbers of Atlantic salmon do spawn in East Coast tributaries as far south as Connecticut, much of the fish's native southern habitat has been destroyed by dams, pollution, and development. Today, the heaviest runs of Atlantic salmon occur from Maine northward along the Canadian coast to the far northern reaches of Quebec. Photograph © Mark Giovanetti/ProPhoto

During the spawning migration, male sockeye salmon aggressively battle for the right to spawn with a female. By the time they reach the spawning grounds, the sockeye's flesh is often ripped and cut by the wicked jaws of its competitors. Their journey is a life-and-death struggle that ultimately ends with the death of one generation and the birth of a new one. Photograph © William H. Mullins

SOCKEYE SALMON

The most abundant Pacific salmon is the sockeye or red salmon, *Oncorhynchus nerka*. Millions of sockeyes pack Pacific Coast tributaries each year on their spawning run, making them easy targets for sport anglers and commercial netters.

At sea, the sockeye looks much like the chinook and coho salmon with its blue-green back and silver body, but during the spawning run, extreme changes turn the sockeye into a completely different creature: The head and tail turn green, the rest of the body changes to bright red, and—in males—the back becomes crudely humped and the jaw hooks wickedly. Spawning adults begin their migration in the summer, usually selecting tributaries that connect to lakes. The fish travel hundreds of miles to reach their spawning grounds by the fall. When spring arrives and the sockeye eggs hatch, the parr move to the lake where they feed heavily for about a year before moving out to sea.

Although it plays a more important role as a commercial fish than as a game fish, the sockeye is pursued by some anglers. Small for a Pacific salmon, the sockeye averages only 5 or 6 pounds (2.3 or 2.7 kg),

The pink salmon earned the nickname humpback, or humpy, because breeding males, like this one caught in the Susitna River in Alaska, develop a humped back during its spawning run. The male pink salmon's transformation from a sleek, silver fish to a wickedly humped monster is one of the most dramatic changes among breeding Pacific salmon. Photograph © Robert E. Barber

though anglers have reeled in trophies weighing more than 10 pounds (4.5 kg).

The sockeye's native range extended from the Arctic drainages of northern Alaska, south along the Pacific Coast to northern California. Attempts to transplant the sockeye to other regions of North America have not fared well, but the landlocked subspecies, known as the kokonee salmon, *Oncorhynchus nerka kennerlyi*, has been introduced with some success to northern lakes as far east as Maine. Averaging less than 2 pounds (.9 kg), the kokonee follows the life cycle of its Pacific Coast relatives, living most of its life in a lake before migrating to a tributary to spawn and die.

PINK SALMON

The smallest of the Pacific salmon is the pink salmon, *Oncorhynchus gorbuscha*. Like the sockeye, the pink salmon's size limits its popularity, and it is more highly prized by commercial netters than sport anglers.

Pink salmon, the smallest of the Pacific salmon, fight their way through extremely shallow water in their quest to reach the spawning grounds. Shallow water is just one of many natural hazards the fish face during their journey upstream. In this case, the pink salmon's drive to complete their mission is greater than the hazard before them. Photograph © Michael Quinton

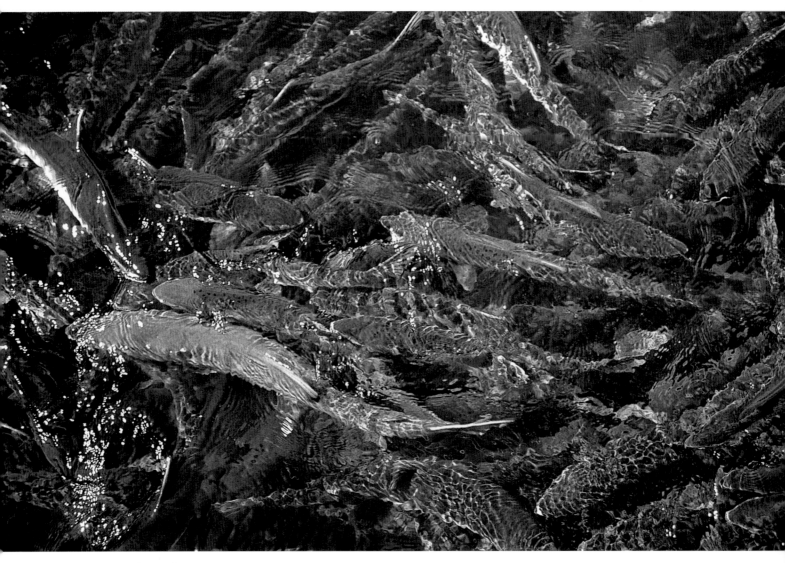

Hundreds of thousands of chum salmon clog rivers where spawning runs are the heaviest. The chum salmon's nickname of dog salmon is said to have originated from native peoples who fed chum salmon to their dogs. Others say the chum is called the dog salmon because its teeth enlarge dramatically during the spawn making the fish look like a dog. Photograph © Ron Sanford

However, its scrappy nature and delicious meat are consolation enough for some anglers to keep pursuing the little salmon.

The pink is a two-year salmon—a key reason it does not reach the sizes of its immense cousins. An average pink weighs about 2 or 3 pounds (.9 to 1.4 kg), but anglers have caught pinks weighing more than 10 pounds (4.5 kg).

At sea, the pink is blue-green above and silver below, resembling its cousins the chinook, coho, and sockeye. During the spawning run, both males and females develop a red to brown stripe running lengthwise down the middle of the side. The pink is nicknamed the humpback after the grotesque hump that develops on the back of the breeding male.

The pink salmon, which spawns in the fall, usually has a much shorter spawning migration than its cousins of the Pacific. In some cases, the pink may travel less than 1 mile (1.6 km) to reach its spawning grounds. Pink salmon eggs, which number as many as two thousand, hatch in the spring, and the young move out to the sea or lake a short time after hatching.

The native range of the pink salmon included an area from the Arctic drainages of the Northwest Territory and Alaska, south along the Pacific Cost to northern California. Transplanted accidentally to Lake Superior in the late 1950s, the pink has thrived in the upper Great Lakes. It also has been introduced to waters in Newfoundland.

CHUM SALMON

Of the five Pacific salmon species, the chum or dog salmon, *Oncorhynchus keta*, plays the smallest role as a game fish. Although it averages about 10 or 15 pounds (4.5 or 6.8 kg), and can exceed 20 pounds (9 kg), anglers often pass the chum over in favor of more popular or larger salmon species. By contrast, the chum is valued as a commercial fish and also as food for birds and animals.

In the ocean, the chum has a blue back and silvery body, but during the spawning migration, the fish turns olive with red to maroon blotches on its sides. The male develops a hooked jaw and enlarged teeth.

Like its cousins of the Pacific Coast, the chum salmon spawns in the fall. The fish usually migrates less than 1 mile (1.6 km) to its breeding site, though the natural features of some rivers demand the chum salmon travel many miles to reach spawning grounds. The eggs incubate on the gravel bottom until spring; the young move to sea soon after hatching.

The chum's native range included most of Alaska, the McKenzie and Anderson river drainages in the Northwest Territory, and the Pacific Coast as far south as central California.

Chapter 5

BULLHEAD CATFISH

Often spurned by mainstream anglers who prefer more glamorous game fish species, catfish are widely misunderstood. Viewed by some as dirty, undesirable, and whiskered bottom feeders, these unique game fish in actuality fight aggressively when hooked and provide first-class table fare. Those anglers who understand the virtues of catfish angling take their sport seriously, because they realize catfish are among the toughest and largest game fish in North America. Take for instance, the blue catfish, king of the catfish species. The world record weighed 14 pounds more than the world record chinook salmon, making the blue catfish one of the most enormous game fish to roam North America's freshwaters.

Found throughout much of the United States and southern Canada, catfish have their most deeply rooted following among anglers in the South and Midwest. The sport is catching on, however, in regions where catfish anglers were virtually nonexistent years ago, as more and more anglers discover the thrill of hooking one of these powerful fish.

Catfish and their cousins the bullheads belong to the *Ictaluridae* family, the largest family of freshwater fish in the United States, though only a fraction of its forty species are considered game fish. *Ictaluridae* species are characterized by the eight barbels, or whiskers, around their mouths. Shaped like a teardrop when viewed from above, their bodies taper from a wide, flat head to a thin tail. Their skin is smooth and lacks scales, and sharp, protective spines capable of cutting an angler's

~≈~

Members of the bullhead catfish family, like this brown bullhead, are among the easiest species of North America's game fish to recognize. Their scaleless skin and four pairs of whisker-like barbels make bullhead catfish stand out from other game fish species. Bullhead catfish belong to the Ictaluridae *family, which includes more than forty species of freshwater fish in North America.* Photograph © Rob & Ann Simpson

hand are found in the dorsal, pectoral, and pelvic abdominal fins.

The "whiskers" on catfish and bullheads (as on cats) intensify their senses of touch and smell. Bottom feeders, catfish and bullheads rely on these senses to identify potential prey. Barbels are used in combination with the fish's lateral lines, which sense water vibrations from prey, making catfish and bullheads effective feeders at night and in murky water.

The blue catfish is one of the largest game fish in North America's freshwaters. Throughout its range, the blue catfish goes by various nicknames, including blue channel, highfin blue, chucklehead cat, great blue cat, forktail cat, humpback blue, and Mississippi cat. The term furcatus *in the blue catfish's scientific name means "forked" in Latin, and refers to the fish's forked tail.* Photograph © Keith Sutton

BLUE CATFISH

Among the largest of the catfish, and one of the largest freshwater game fish in North America, is the blue catfish, *Ictalurus furcatus*. The official world record, caught by William P. McKinley in the Wheeler Reservoir in Alabama in 1996, weighed-in at 111 pounds (50.35 kg), but stories of blues weighing over 150 pounds (68 kg) are told throughout the bait stores and bars of the Lower Mississippi River drainages. On average, blue catfish tip the scales at 12 or 13 pounds (5.4 or 5.9 kg).

Named for its blue back, the blue catfish sports white to silver-blue lower fins and chin barbels. Small blue catfish usually are pale blue with a white underside, while larger members of the species are darker with a silver-blue underside. One way to distinguish the blue catfish from other catfish species is to examine the anal fin: The blue catfish has an anal fin with a straight, even edge, while other catfish species have anal fins with rounded edges.

The blue catfish's native range extended through the Mississippi River drainages south of Minnesota. It included the Missouri River as far north as South Dakota, and the Ohio River as far north as Pennsylvania. It also is native to the drainages of the Rio Grande in southern Texas, southern New Mexico, and northern Mexico. Transplantation expanded blue catfish angling opportunities to a few areas outside its native range, mainly in the western and Atlantic United States. Within parts of the blue catfish's native range, populations have decreased because of the construction of dams and other development, which hamper the fish's migratory movements.

Living in schools, blue catfish most often reside in the clear water of main channels or backwaters of medium or large rivers, or in the deepest water of reservoirs, commonly over a mud, pebble, or sand bottom. The fish feed by swimming along the bottom searching for their main food sources of fish and crayfish.

Spawning

In June or July when the water temperature reaches 80°F (27°C), adult blue catfish move to protected areas in shallow water to spawn. In some cases they migrate as far as 100 miles (160 km) to reach the spawning grounds. The female, which reaches sexual maturity at age four or five, deposits her eggs in a nest made by the male or uses existing cover such as logs or root tangles as a nest. A 20-pound (9-kg) female may lay as many as sixty thousand eggs, which the waiting male fertilizes.

After the spawn is complete, the female leaves the nesting site, and the male remains behind to guard the eggs and, later, the young fry.

CHANNEL CATFISH

A wide range and willingness to take a variety of baits has made the channel catfish, *Ictalurus punctatus*, a favorite among catfish anglers. Although it closely resembles the blue catfish, the channel cat does not grow as large as its cousin. The channel catfish has a pale blue to gray

In muddy or stained water, the channel catfish uses its barbels and sense of smell to locate food. The channel cat feeds on a variety of prey, including small fish, snails, crayfish, and aquatic insects, and is more willing than its cousins to eat dead prey. Photograph © Mark Giovanetti/ProPhoto

The channel catfish bears a close resemblance to its cousin the blue catfish. One way to differentiate between the two species is to count the anal rays. A channel catfish has twenty-four to twenty-nine rays on its anal fin, while the blue catfish's anal fin has thirty or more rays.
Photograph © Keith Sutton

back, white to silvery sides, and a white belly, so casual observation does not allow novices to differentiate between the two species. Closer examination reveals dark spots on the channel catfish's back and a rounded edge to its anal fin, which the blue catfish lacks. An average channel catfish weighs between 2 and 5 pounds (.9 to 2.3 kg), but the world record, caught by W. B. Whaley in the Santee-Cooper Reservoir in South Carolina in 1964, tipped the scales at 58 pounds (26.31 kg). Netters have hauled in huge channel catfish weighing more than 70 pounds (32 kg).

The channel cat's native range extended from northern Montana to southern Quebec in the North, and from north-central Mexico to southern Florida in the South. Stocking and transplantation efforts have expanded its range from coast to coast.

Although it does inhabit lakes, reservoirs, and streams, the channel catfish is most fond of the clear, moving water of large to medium rivers and prefers a clean bottom of sand, gravel, or rocks. During the daylight hours, the channel catfish remains inactive, hiding in tree roots, near dams, or in deep holes. At sundown, schools of channel cats move into shallow water, feeding on the bottom and attacking small fish, crayfish, and aquatic insects. Unlike other catfish species, the channel catfish occasionally rises to take insects from the water's surface.

In contrast to other game fish such as the walleye or northern pike, which seek out cool water during the hottest days of summer, the channel catfish remains active in temperatures as warm as 90°F (32°C). In the winter, the channel cat seeks out a protected area in deep water, where it remains sedentary until temperatures warm in the spring.

Spawning

In the late spring to early summer, when water temperatures are between 75°F and 80°F (24°C and 27°C), channel catfish move to their spawning sites in tributaries. The female selects a protected, well-oxygenated area among logs or tree roots to lay her eggs. The male clears the area of silt by fanning his body over the nest. After depositing as many as twenty thousand adhesive eggs, the female leaves the spawning area. The male fertilizes the eggs and stays on the nest to protect the eggs until they hatch one to two weeks later. When the fry hatch, the male stays with the school of young to guard them from predators.

FLATHEAD CATFISH

Like the blue and channel cats, the flathead catfish, *Pylodictis olivaris*, is capable of growing to enormous sizes. Although the ones landed with rod and reel are usually in the neighborhood of 5 to 10 pounds (2.3 to 4.5 kg), commercial netters have hauled in flatheads weighing more than 100 pounds (45 kg). The world record caught by Ken Paulie in Elk City Reservoir, Kansas, in 1998 weighed an amazing 123 pounds (55.79 kg).

A member of the *Ameiurus* genus, the flathead bears little resemblance to the blue or channel catfish, both of which belong to the *Ictalurus* genus. Named for its collapsed, wide head, the flathead has a black to olive-brown upper body, black to brown blotches on the sides, and a yellow to white belly. Other distinguishing features include rounded edges on the tail and a large adipose fin.

The flathead is native to an area extending from central North Dakota to western Pennsylvania in the North, and from northern Mexico to Mississippi in the South. Sporadic introductions outside its native range have modestly increased its accessibility to anglers.

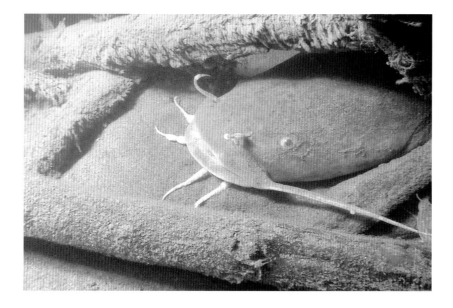

Adult flathead catfish are solitary fish that, during the daytime, hide in protected areas among roots, weeds, and other cover. In the evening, flatheads emerge from hiding and make their way to shallow water, where they feed heavily on a variety of aquatic life throughout the night. Photograph © Doug Stamm/ProPhoto

Quiet backwaters or pools of small to large rivers are the flathead's preferred habitat, where it hides in the tangles of roots or log jams, waiting for passing minnows, crayfish, or aquatic insects. In some parts of its range, flatheads also live in lakes and reservoirs with similar cover.

When the blazing heat of summer raises water temperatures to levels unbearable for many game fish species, the flathead, like its cousins, remains unfazed. Active in water as warm as the low 90s (32°C to 34°C), the flathead's metabolism slows to near hibernation levels during the winter months when it seeks refuge in deep water among the protection of logs or tree roots and remains inactive until spring.

Spawning

The flathead spawns in the late spring or early summer, when water temperatures are in the low to mid-70s (21°C to 25°C). The female, which reaches sexual maturity at age five, lays the eggs on a submerged log or in a root tangle. The male fertilizes the eggs, then both parents remain with the eggs and newly hatched fry to protect them from predators.

Anglers do most of their fishing for monster flathead catfish during the nighttime hours. Anglers in some regions refer to the flathead as the yellow cat, because the fish usually is yellow, yellowish-brown, light brown, or olive on its back and sides. Its underside is yellow- or cream-colored. The Latin term olivaris *in the flathead's scientific name means "olive-colored."* Photograph © Keith Sutton

WHITE CATFISH

Countless children in the eastern United States spend their summers catching white catfish, *Ameiurus catus*. The smallest of North America's four main catfish species, the white catfish still puts up a good fight when hooked. Its size limits its appeal for many adult anglers, but for kids it ranks right up there in popularity with panfish like sunfish and crappies. A typical white catfish weighs 1 pound (.45 kg) or less, but occasionally anglers take specimens weighing more than 5 pounds (2.3 kg). The world record caught by James Robinson at the William Land Park Pond in California in 1994 weighed an impressive 22 pounds (9.98 kg).

Blue-black to blue-gray coloring above and white to yellow below, the white catfish has white chin barbels and a moderately forked tail. It lives in slow-moving rivers with muddy bottoms and tolerates murkier and more polluted water than other catfish species. Small fish, crustaceans, and insects are the staples of its diet.

The white catfish is native to the Atlantic Coast states from New

White catfish feed primarily on small fish, but their omnivorous diets also consist of crustaceans, aquatic insects, fish eggs, and aquatic plants. In contrast to the flathead, channel, and blue catfish, who feed primarily at night, white catfish often feed during the day. Photograph © Doug Stamm/ ProPhoto

York, south through Florida, and the Gulf states to Mississippi. Extensive stocking and transplantation extended its range across much of the United States, and today it is found as far west as California.

Spawning

White catfish spawn in the late spring to early summer, with males and females working together to fan out a nest with their bodies. The female deposits her two thousand to four thousand eggs in the carefully prepared nest, then the male releases his cloud of milt over the eggs. Both parents remain on the nest to protect eggs and fry from predators, leaving when the young fish disperse from their school.

HEADWATER CATFISH

Catfish anglers in southern Texas and southern New Mexico are familiar with the headwater catfish, *Ictalurus lupus*. Although nearly identical in appearance to the channel catfish, the headwater cat is a separate, distinct species. Its body coloring is similar to its cousin's, with a pale blue back and a white to silver lower side. Two distinguishing features are the head and mouth, which are wider than the channel cat's. It also is a smaller fish, averaging about 1 pound (.45 kg).

The headwater catfish is common within its limited range, which is restricted to parts of the Rio Grande drainages in southern New Mexico, southern Texas and northern Mexico.

The headwater catfish seeks out the clear water of small rivers and creeks with a sand or gravel bottom, and prefers cooler water than other catfish species.

YELLOW BULLHEAD

For many adults, the yellow bullhead, *Ameiurus natalis*, along with North America's other bullhead species, is just a pest, hooked while fishing for more alluring fish. For children, though, catching a bullhead is one of the true joys of summer. The fish's scrappy, hard-fighting nature (along with the added thrill of its razor-sharp dorsal and pectoral spines), sends generation after generation of kids to the local pond or lake to do battle with bullheads. Add to that the excellent flavor of their meat, and bullheads become classic game fish for North America's young anglers.

As its name implies, the yellow bullhead is a yellow-tinted fish; it has a yellow belly and a yellowish tinge to its olive-brown to black back and sides. Like all bullheads, it has a rounded edge to its tail. The yellow bullhead can be distinguished from its cousins by its chin barbels, which are white or yellow, rather than black or brown. On average, it is one of the largest bullhead species, typically weighing about ¾ pound (.34 kg).

Most ponds and lakes in the area stretching from North Dakota to southern Quebec in the North, and from Texas to southern Florida in the South, hold populations of yellow bullheads. In many cases, the yellow bullhead and its brown and black counterparts are the only game fish to inhabit ponds and small lakes that typically experience winterkill or have regularly low oxygen levels. The yellow bullhead, though,

The yellow bullhead, like its cousins the brown and black bullheads, may quickly overpopulate a pond, lake, or stream if too few predators are around to keep its numbers in check. Bodies of water with high bullhead populations can provide unlimited action for anglers, because the fish are easy to locate and willing to eat a wide variety of prey. Photograph © Bill Vaznis/The Green Agency

prefers clearer water than its cousins, and usually does not inhabit murky or extremely dirty water.

All bullhead species spawn in the late spring to early summer. Eggs are laid in shallow water on a mud or sand bottom, and the parents remain on the nest to protect the eggs and fry. When the school of fry begins moving around in search of food, the parents herd their young to guard them from predators.

BROWN BULLHEAD

Named for its blotchy brown back and sides, the brown bullhead, *Ameiurus nebulosus*, has a white to yellow-brown underside, long, dark chin barbels, and a square edge to its tail. An average brown bullhead weighs between ½ and ¾ pound (.23 and .34 kg).

The brown bullhead is indigenous to an area stretching from southeastern Saskatchewan to New Brunswick in the North, and from northern Louisiana to southern Florida in the South. Transplantation has

In some parts of its range, brown bullhead have a poor image, having been unjustly labeled as dirty bottom feeders. In truth, the brown bullhead is a scrappy game fish that makes a tasty meal. In fact, in some areas of the southern United States, brown bullheads are raised commercially for their meat. Photograph © Patrice Ceisel/Shedd Aquarium

expanded its range to include most of the United States.

While it does live in small lakes and ponds, the brown bullhead is more likely to inhabit larger lakes, streams, and rivers. It feeds on small fish, invertebrates, and aquatic insects.

BLACK BULLHEAD

Of the three main bullhead species, the black bullhead, *Amelurus melas*, tolerates the most oxygen-poor waters. It often inhabits muddy ponds, sluggish streams, and small lakes where winterkill is an annual occurrence.

The black bullhead has a black to dark brown back, brown to olive sides, and a white to yellow underside. Its chin barbels are dark, and its tail has a square edge. One distinguishing feature that separates the black bullhead from the brown or yellow bullhead are the edges of the pectoral fins: Both the yellow and brown bullhead have saw-like, serrated edges to their pectoral fins, while the edges of the black bullheads' pectoral fins are rough but without serrations. On average, the black bullhead weighs about ¾ pound (.34 kg).

The native range of the black bullhead extended from southern Saskatchewan to western New York in the North, and from northeastern Mexico to western Georgia in the South. It is now found throughout most of the United States, due to extensive transplantation.

On average, black bullheads live four or five years and rarely grow larger than 1 pound (.45 kg). In very rare cases, they may live as long as ten years and weigh 5 pounds (2.3 kg) or more. The world record black bullhead caught by Charles M. Taylor at Sturgis Pond, Michigan, in 1987 weighed 8 pounds, 15 ounces (4.04 kg). Photograph © Gary Meszaros/Visuals Unlimited

Chapter 6

PERCH

M illions of anglers consider the walleye the jewel of all game fish. In my home state, hundreds of thousands of anglers are drawn to Minnesota's walleye lakes on opening day of the season, making it one of North America's premier fishing events. In many regions of the northern United States and Canada, walleye far exceed all other game fish in popularity; Minnesota anglers alone take home about 3.5 million walleyes each year.

Although the walleye and its cousins the sauger and perch are not particularly beautiful fish, they have captured the hearts of anglers with their cooperative nature and exquisite taste.

The walleye, sauger, and yellow perch are the three game fish species from the *Percidae* or perch family, which includes 153 species, and boasts North America's second most diverse family of fish, after catfish. All three are cool-water species with native ranges that stretched over much of Canada and the north-central and central United States, east of the Rocky Mountains. Dramatic range increases due to stocking have played an important role in their climb toward the top of North America's list of most popular game fish.

Compared to other game fish species such as the black bass, northern pike, muskellunge, or trout, perch are not tenacious or powerful fish. They are, however, efficient predators, willing to strike a variety of prey—a great assistance to an angler. Another key factor in their accessibility is their communal nature: Perch, unlike most of North America's top freshwater game fish species, are schooling fish,

The walleye is the largest member of the Percidae *or perch family. Anglers gravitate toward the walleye because it is an aggressive feeder, is fairly easy to locate, and makes an exceptional meal. Thanks to extensive transplantation during the twentieth century, walleyes are currently found in forty states and nearly every Canadian province.* Photograph © Jack Bissell

often easier to locate than solitary species.

Perch inhabit the calm pools or backwaters of rivers and streams, ponds, lakes, and reservoirs.

WALLEYE

A trip to Mille Lacs Lake in north-central Minnesota, imprints an indelible image on a visitor's memory. Here the walleye, *Stizostedion vitreum*, holds an almost mythical place in the minds of anglers. Life revolves around the yearly life cycle of the walleye. In the spring, residents and local businesses prepare for May's walleye opener and the migration of thousands of anglers to the area; a movement which plays a major role in supporting the local economy. Throughout the summer and fall anglers trek to this renowned walleye lake in droves to pursue their favorite fish. When the lake ices over in December, a new wave of anglers arrives, bringing ice houses and augers to fish for walleyes through the frozen surface.

The walleye's popularity is not as extreme everywhere the fish is found, but it does have a large and loyal following across northern and central North America. Originally inhabiting a range extending from the Northwest Territory to Quebec in the North, and from northern Colorado to northern Georgia in the South, its range has broadened through stocking. Today, the walleye can also be found in areas of the Pacific, Atlantic, and Gulf drainages; it is a cool-water species and cannot tolerate excessively warm waters like those of Florida. The heart of walleye country is the Great Lakes region, where stocking, management, and fishing pressure are heavy.

The largest member of the perch family, the walleye belongs to the subspecies *leucopercids*. It name derives from its eerie eyes, which are large, staring, and silvery. Covered with a layer of opaque tissue that gathers light, the fish's specialized eyes allow it to see and pursue prey in low-light conditions. It has a brassy-brown, cigar-shaped body, which is dark above and white below, with dark brown patches on the upper half. Its mouth is large and filled with sharp teeth. The walleye looks similar

The walleye has distinctive brassy yellow scales on its sides, giving it a tarnished-metal appearance. Between five and twelve large dark blotches on its back break up these yellow scales. Anglers who take the time to count will find the walleye has between 77 and 104 scales along its lateral line. Photograph © Bill Buckley/The Green Agency

Walleyes are most often found in clear lakes and rivers with rocky or gravel bottoms, where they congregate near structures, such as submerged brush or trees, rock piles, aquatic plants, and steep drop-offs. Walleyes will feed during any time of the day or night, but avoid direct sunlight because their specialized eyes are very sensitive to light. They feed most heavily during the hours surrounding sunrise and sunset. Photograph © Mark Giovanetti/ProPhoto

Walleyes typically spawn in less than 10 feet (3 m) of water in a tributary stream or windblown shallows, where eggs receive proper aeration. After the spawning ritual, walleyes move out to deeper water, sometimes more than 30 feet (9 m) deep. Their feeding picks up substantially after the spawn, when they feed minimally or not at all. Photograph © Bill Vaznis/The Green Agency

to the sauger, except the walleye has a black spot on its first dorsal fin and a white spot on both its anal fin and tail. The world record walleye caught by Al Nelson at Greer's Ferry Lake, Alabama, in 1982 weighed a whopping 22 pounds, 11 ounces (10.29 kg), but the average walleye weighs between 1 and 3 pounds (.45 and 1.4 kg). Females commonly outlive and outweigh males.

Night Vision

The specialized eyes of a walleye make it an efficient predator: It uses its excellent vision to ambush prey such as smaller fish that cannot see well in low-light conditions. Although it can and does feed during any hour of the day or night, the walleye's peak feeding times are during the early morning and evening, when light is low and prey is on the move. During these peak feeding times, schools of walleye move from their daytime deepwater holding areas to shallower water, where they feed on prey such as yellow perch and other small fish, crayfish, and insects. During the day, the walleye usually takes cover away from the light among weeds, rocks, or other structure, or in deep water. Factors that lower light levels, such as cloud cover, murky water, or a windswept surface, often bring the walleye out of its daytime cover to feed. Walleyes that live in turbulent rivers have a higher level of daytime activity than those that live in lakes or calm rivers.

Spawning

In early spring, when the days start to warm and the ice is receding from lakes and rivers, walleyes make their first movements of spawning activity. While water temperatures are still in the mid-30s (1°C to 3°C), the males, which reach sexual maturity by their second or third year, begin moving toward the spawning areas. As temperatures creep closer to the 40s (4°C to 9°C), the females, which reach sexual maturity at age four or five, follow. For successful reproduction, walleyes need shallow water with a rock or gravel bottom. Their favorite spawning area is a tributary stream or river, where the current can aerate eggs and keep them free from sediment. When water temperatures reach a range from 43°F to 50°F (6°C to 10°C), the fish are ready to spawn. Like most of the walleye's activity, spawning takes place during low-light conditions. In the period of one to two days, a female deposits between twenty-five thousand and seven hundred thousand eggs, depending on her size. Males are capable of spawning with several females in a similar time frame.

The walleye displays spawning activity for about a week. After the fish have spawned, both males and females leave the spawning area, abandoning the eggs. With no parental protection, both eggs and fry are vulnerable to predators, yet they face an even greater threat in cold weather. The walleye is a prolific species, but low temperatures during egg and fry development can have a devastating affect on reproductive success. Cold weather can both hamper the hatch and delay the development of tiny organisms that fry need to feed upon.

If the eggs survive, they hatch in a span of one to three weeks. Fry school up and move away from the spawning grounds, feeding first on tiny zooplankton, then graduating to larger organisms as they grow. By fall, the young reach about 5 inches (13 cm) in length.

Habitat

Whether living in the Arctic drainage, Gulf drainage, or any point in between, the walleye is most often found in large lakes and rivers. An ideal walleye lake is cool, clear, expansive, and shallow with a rocky or sandy bottom and plenty of structure. A large river or stream with cool, slow-moving water and deep pools also makes for excellent walleye habitat. The walleye can adapt to a less than ideal habitat like small eutrophic lakes, but it does require water temperatures in the 60s and 70s (16°C to 26°C), and a prolonged period of temperatures below 50°F (10°C) for proper egg development.

In spring, after spawning, the walleye spends much of its time in shallow water, feeding heavily to regain energy lost during the spawn. As spring progresses into summer and water temperatures rise, walleyes spend more time in cooler, deeper water, coming into warmer shallow water in the early morning and evening to feed. It may also hide in deeper water to prey on schools of baitfish.

As water temperatures fall, the walleye's metabolism slows down. In late autumn it moves into shallow water and remains there to feed until after the water freezes over. As winter progresses and vegetation begins to decompose, the walleye moves to deeper water in search of higher oxygen levels and baitfish that are moving out to other areas in search of food. Although a cool-water species, the walleye remains chiefly inactive during the winter months, staying near the bottom and feeding about once every twenty days.

SAUGER

Although it resembles the walleye in many ways, the sauger, *Stizostedion canadense*, rates lower in popularity than its cousin. In a few areas of North America the sauger is a popular species, and thus plays an important role in the game fish community. More often though, the sauger shares habitat with, and becomes overshadowed by, its larger relative.

Distribution is the key factor limiting the sauger's popularity. Its native range included an area from western Alberta to eastern Quebec in the North, and from northern Louisiana to northern Alabama in the South. Its range has expanded through stocking to include parts of the Atlantic and Gulf drainages, but the sauger's habitat is limited within its range. In addition to requiring cool water with a rock or gravel bottom, the sauger needs big lakes and rivers. In some cases, it has adapted to smaller waters, but, unlike the walleye, the sauger is not tolerant to stocking in waters outside its preferred habitat. In Minnesota, for example, the sauger lives almost exclusively in sections of the state's largest lakes and rivers, inhabiting only a tiny fraction of the more than seventeen hundred lakes and three thousand rivers and streams that the walleye calls home.

In parts of its range, the sauger goes by the nicknames sand pike and sand pickerel, though it is of no relation to either the northern pike or pickerel. The sauger's closest relative is the walleye. The two fish share habitats in many areas, but the walleye, which grows considerably larger, receives the majority of anglers' attention. Photograph © Doug Stamm/ProPhoto

The sauger's size also limits its appeal as a game fish. While a 3-pound (1.4-kg) walleye is common, a similar sized sauger is a rarity. A 6-pounder (2.7-kilogrammer) is an exceptional catch indeed. The world record caught by Mike Fisher in North Dakota's Lake Sakakawea in 1971 weighed-in at 8 pounds, 12 ounces (3.97 kg).

With a few distinguishing exceptions, the sauger looks much like the walleye. It is dark brassy-brown above and brassy-yellow on the sides with a whitish belly. However, the three to four dark spots on its back and sides are darker and more definite than the walleye's, and its body is more streamlined. Also, the sauger's spiny dorsal fins bear rows of small black spots, and neither its anal fin nor tail bear a white spot. The sauger does share the eerie silvery eyes of its cousin, and its eyesight is even better than the walleye's in low-light conditions.

YELLOW PERCH

Widespread, prolific, and cooperative, the yellow perch, *Perca flavescens*, holds a special place in the hearts of many North American anglers because it was the first fish they hooked as a child.

Commonly included in the vast spectrum of game fish labeled panfish, the ubiquitous yellow perch plays a dual role in the North American game fish ecosystem. To anglers, the little yellow perch is a great panfish—easy to catch, tasty, and small enough to fry whole in a pan. To large fish such as the walleye, northern pike, black bass, and muskie, the yellow perch is a key source of food. Throughout much of its range, the walleye is dependent on the yellow perch as a meal. The walleye's dependency is so great in some areas that a poor year class of perch can negatively affect the larger fish's populations.

The yellow perch's native range stretched from the Northwest Territory to Nova Scotia in the North, and from eastern Nebraska to Maryland, down the Atlantic Coast through Virginia and the Carolinas in the South. Like the walleye, the yellow perch was successfully transplanted across a large portion of the United States and Canada. Within its range, the yellow perch inhabits much of the same water as walleye, as well as the same habitat within a lake or river, thus accounting for the pair's relationship as predator and prey.

Bearing little resemblance to its cousins the walleye and sauger, the yellow perch is easy to identify. Its deep, chunky body is dark green above and white to whitish-yellow below, with golden yellow sides. It has six to eight dark vertical bars on its sides and orange pectoral, pelvic, and anal fins. Its mouth is large like its cousins', but lacks the rows of large sharp teeth. The world record yellow perch caught by Dr. C. C. Abbot in the Delaware River at Bordentown, New Jersey, in 1865 weighed 4 pounds, 3 ounces (1.90 kg); on average the fish weighs less than ½ pound (.23 kg).

The yellow perch lacks the excellent low-light vision of the walleye

The smaller cousin of the walleye and sauger, the yellow perch plays a dual role among game fish. On one hand, it is an important food source for larger fish such as walleyes, northern pike, and muskies. On the other hand, the yellow perch is a scrappy, great-tasting panfish many anglers love to catch. Photograph © Doug Stamm/ProPhoto

Throughout the Great Lakes region, the yellow perch becomes a popular game fish during the winter, especially during the late winter months when walleye and northern pike seasons are closed. On a lake with an abundant yellow perch population, an angler can pull one hundred or more fish through the ice in a day. Photograph © Bill Vaznis/The Green Agency

and sauger, so most of its activity takes place during the daytime. Its eyesight is a weakness during the low-light hours of morning and evening, when the walleye and sauger move in and can easily prey on schools of yellow perch. During the day, other large species such as the northern and muskie feed on yellow perch.

Yellow perch live in schools made up of fish of similar age and size, numbering as many as two hundred. The schools remain in a relatively contained area throughout the year, feeding on small fish, insects, and crustaceans.

Spawning

In spring, when water temperatures begin to warm, nature calls the yellow perch to its spawning grounds. It often will migrate miles to find the right spawning area. Like the walleye, it prefers a tributary stream or shallow water with a rock or gravel bottom.

Males, which reach sexual maturity at age one or two, arrive at the spawning grounds first. The female, which is able to breed at age two, arrives soon after. Spawning activity takes place when the water temperature ranges from the mid-40s to the low 50s (6°C to 11°C). A female deposits up to fifty thousand eggs in a random area, and as many as twenty males fertilize the eggs. After spawning, the parents quickly abandon the eggs.

The fry hatch in eight to ten days and begin feeding on tiny zooplankton. They eventually graduate to larger food sources, such as small fish, crustaceans, and insects. Young yellow perch are extremely vulnerable to predators and only a tiny fraction of those hatched survive the first year.

Chapter 7

PIKE

Two of the largest, most aggressive game fish species in North America's freshwaters, the northern pike and muskellunge are true trophy species. Anglers who seriously pursue these powerful predators are the big game hunters of fishing. Collectively, they spend millions of dollars each year traveling to trophy waters in search of bigger specimens to mount on their walls or add to their photo or video albums.

The northern and muskie are fierce fighters at the end of a line and do not surrender easily. The pair belong to the *Esocidae* family, which also includes the grass or redfin pickerel and the chain pickerel. Characteristics shared by *Esocidae* members include a long, torpedo-shaped body and a duck bill–like mouth filled with rows of needle-sharp teeth. Each species has a single spineless dorsal fin located near the back of the body.

The aggressive nature and strength of *Esocidae* species are key factors in their popularity, but their range and prevalence also contribute to their importance as game fish species. The northern pike, for example, inhabits a large portion of the northern United States, Alaska, and most of Canada. The abundance of most *Esocidae* species within their ranges makes them fairly easy to locate.

To reach trophy size, northern pike need specific conditions, including cool, well-oxygenated water, a strong base of food such as yellow perch or white suckers, and restrictive regulations or a remote location that protect larger fish from heavy angling pressure. Without these conditions, small northern pike commonly overpopulate a lake or river, making larger northerns scarce or nonexistent. Photograph © Bill Vaznis/The Green Agency

NORTHERN PIKE

In most of the waters it inhabits, the northern pike, *Esox lucius*, reigns as king of the food pyramid. Long, sleek, and intimidating, the northern is an efficient, fearless hunter. Any creature that moves within the ecosystem of a lake or river can fall victim to its powerful jaws. Small fish such as minnows, sunfish, perch, and suckers are common prey for the northern; other unfortunates such as frogs, salamanders, crayfish, leeches, ducklings, baby muskrats, and mice also are on its menu of potential meals. Even larger fish, such as the black bass and walleye, risk becoming the northern's dinner.

The northern's muscular body is colored dark green above and white below with brassy green sides. Rows of white to yellow worm-shaped markings run along its sides from head to tail. Dark green spots and lines streak its yellow to red fins. It has yellow eyes, a large tooth-filled mouth, and rounded edges on its tail. Although the northern is capable of living more than twelve years and growing in excess of 40 pounds (18 kg), a typical northern catch is about three to six years old and weighs less than 10 pounds (4.5 kg). Where fishing pressure is extremely heavy, an average northern may weigh only 3 pounds (1.4 kg). The world record caught by Peter Dubuc at the Sacandaga Reservoir in New York in 1940 weighed 46 pounds, 2 ounces (20.92 kg).

The northern's native North American range extended from the Arctic drainages of Alaska to Labrador in the North, and from Oklahoma to Pennsylvania in the South. Introduction has expanded its range

Anglers who pursue northern pike are chasing one of the continent's strongest and most vicious freshwater fish. In most waters they inhabit, northern pike sit atop the food chain. They often exhibit an inflated fearlessness that causes them to strike at nearly any object moving within their territories. Photograph © Bill Buckley/The Green Agency

The northern pike's spawning activity begins in early spring, sometimes before ice-out. If they have access to tributary streams such as small rivers or shallow creeks, northerns commonly travel upstream to spawn. This northern's journey is blocked by a man-made obstacle. Photograph © Bill Vaznis/The Green Agency

to include limited areas of the Rocky Mountain states and parts of Texas, Arkansas, Kentucky, Georgia, and Maine.

Habitat

A cool-water species, the northern prefers a habitat of clear water, with plenty of vegetation. Whether a lake or river, water temperatures must be cool enough for the northern to reach its growth potential. Prolonged temperatures above 70°F (21°C) can have a devastating affect on large northerns, who need well-oxygenated water with temperatures 65°F (18°C) or lower. Although small northerns can tolerate warmer water, big northerns often stop eating and may even perish if water temperatures become too warm.

The northern is a solitary, territorial fish that likes to live under the heavy cover of aquatic weed beds. Depending on sight as its strongest sense, the northern commonly hides along the weedline, waiting to ambush unsuspecting prey or chase competing northerns away. Able to move with short, quick bursts of speed, the northern strikes its prey swiftly and efficiently.

While small northerns spend much of the year in shallow water, large northerns move with the seasons to find preferred water temperatures, oxygenation, and food sources. In the summer, large northerns seek out deep water where temperatures are cooler and the prey is bigger. During the heat of summer, large northerns become sluggish and feeding slows down. As water temperatures cool off in the fall, large northerns move to shallower water, their activity increases, and they feed more heavily. As the heart of winter approaches, large northerns gradually move to deeper water, searching out higher oxygen levels and baitfish. During this period, the northern is more active than other game fish, such as the black bass or walleye, and feeds about once every fifteen to twenty days.

Spawning

As the hours of daylight increase and temperatures begin to warm in early spring, the northern returns to the area where it was born, called back by a homing instinct. This migration often occurs before ice cover is entirely gone. The spawning grounds can be a marshy shallow or a tributary stream or creek. There, spawning-age northerns, those three and older, congregate in preparation for the spawn. When water temperatures reach between 39°F and 52°F (4°C and 11°C), males and females pair off to spawn. The female deposits the eggs in a haphazard fashion and the male fertilizes the eggs; oftentimes a smaller male sneaks in and also fertilizes the eggs. The female takes one to two days to release her approximately one hundred thousand adhesive eggs, which stick to surrounding vegetation. After spawning, both males and females move away from the area to recover, leaving the eggs and fry vulnerable to predators.

After approximately two weeks of development, the northern eggs hatch. In the first few days of life, the fry feed on tiny plankton and

⮌ White Sucker ⮌

Inhabiting much of the same range as the northern pike and muskie, the white sucker, *Catostomus commersoni*, plays an important role as prey for the two game fish species.

This bottom-feeding rough fish inhabits lakes and rivers in a range extending from the Northwest Territory to Newfoundland in the North, and from New Mexico to South Carolina in the South. In northern parts of their ranges, the sucker and the northern pike or muskie are the only non-minnow species found in some lakes, making their predator/prey connection obvious. White suckers commonly overpopulate lakes that do not contain enough predators to control the smaller fish's numbers. In extreme cases, lakes must be chemically reclaimed by fisheries' managers to relieve the problem.

The white sucker feeds by swimming along the bottom, using its suction cup–like mouth to inhale food like aquatic insects, worms, and aquatic plant material. White suckers average 1 to 2 pounds (.45 to .9 kg), occasionally growing as large as 5 or 6 pounds (2.3 or 2.7 kg).

Although not considered a game fish, the white sucker is pursued by some anglers, who use fishing rods, spears, bows, or nets to take them during the spring, when the fish ascend small streams to spawn.

The white sucker belongs to the Catostomus *genus of the* Catostomidae *family. The genus includes more than thirty North American sucker species, of which the white sucker is the most widespread. In all, the* Catostomidae *family boasts more than sixty sucker species.* Photograph © Mark Giovanetti/ProPhoto

invertebrates, then quickly graduate to eating other fish. The aggressive and savage nature of the northern is evident early in life, as fry can turn to eating one another.

Water temperature is an important element in the northern's reproductive success. Northern eggs need near-freezing temperatures to develop properly within a female. Since most lakes and rivers in the warmer climates of the South do not experience those cold temperatures, the northern's range is restricted mainly to Canada and the northern half of the United States.

MUSKELLUNGE

Ask any angler in Hayward, Wisconsin, what the ultimate game fish is, and that person will say, without hesitation, the muskie. Home to the National Fresh Water Fishing Hall of Fame, the north woods town of Hayward houses a five-story artificial muskellunge as part of its downtown museum. The enormous muskellunge, *Esox masquinongy*, is a sign to visitors that they have arrived in muskie country. Muskie fishing and the tourism that accompanies it drive the economy of this small Wisconsin town. Excellent muskie waters surround this area, and the anglers who fish here know a new record could be just a cast away.

Each year, anglers migrate to prime muskie waters in Wisconsin, Minnesota, Michigan, New York, Ontario, and Quebec. The bounty they seek is one of the largest, most powerful game fish in North America's freshwaters.

The muskie, with its long, cylindrical body and large mouth filled with sharp teeth, looks similar to the northern. Its markings, however, are different: Its sides bear dark spots or bars against a light gray to yellowish-green background, its coloring is usually darker on its back, and its belly is white. One sure way of distinguishing a muskie from a northern is to check the number of pores on the fish's lower jaw. The muskie has six or more pores on each side, while the northern has five or fewer. Another clue is the tail: The ends of the northern's tail are rounded, while the muskie's draw to a point.

Although both are capable of growing to enormous sizes, an average northern weighs less than 10 pounds (4.5 kg), and muskies commonly exceed that size. The world record muskie caught by Arthur Lawton in 1957, in the St. Lawrence River in New York, weighed 69 pounds, 15 ounces (31.72 kg).

While the popularity of most North American game fish is tied to the abundance and accessibility of the species, the muskie's is not. It does not have a large range, nor is it abundant compared to most game fish. The muskie's native range extended from southeastern Manitoba to Quebec in the North, and from central Tennessee and northern Georgia to eastern Virginia in the South. Introduction has been only partly

The muskie is one of the fiercest predators to inhabit the freshwaters of North America. Equipped with razor-sharp teeth and a sleek, powerful body, the muskie will eat just about any prey it can strike in or on the water. Stories circulate throughout the Great Lakes region of giant muskies even biting humans swimming in their territory. Photograph © Doug Stamm/ProPhoto

successful in areas outside its native range, and the muskie has not fared well in plantings attempted in the South and the West. The most successful muskie stocking has occurred in new waters within or near its native range.

Habitat

The muskie inhabits lakes, rivers, and streams, usually in cool, clear water around plenty of vegetation. In streams and rivers, it prefers quiet backwaters to areas with strong current. The muskie demands a cool-water environment— excessively warm water can be fatal.

Like its cousin the northern, the muskie feeds heavily on a variety of prey, with smaller fish as its primary food source. Bluegills, perch, suckers, and walleyes are the staples of a muskie's diet, supplemented by other creatures such as frogs, salamanders, crayfish, snakes, baby muskrats, mice, rats, ducklings, and shore birds. Wherever it lives, the muskie stands at the top of the food chain. Any creature that will fit in its giant mouth is a potential meal.

As with large northerns, big muskies' feeding slows down as water temperatures reach their peak in the heat of summer. Their heaviest feeding activity occurs when the water temperature is around 65°F. If temperatures are much warmer than that, feeding slows, and if temperatures approach 80°F (27°C), they may stop feeding altogether.

The muskie is a solitary, stationary fish. Most of a muskie's year is spent in one area in shallow water no more than 20 feet (5 m) deep. Movement to other areas is usually dictated by the need for food. In a river, the muskies may migrate upstream during the summer then back downstream in the fall in search of adequate food sources.

As temperatures cool in the autumn, the muskie's feeding activity increases, yet the muskie is less active during the winter than the northern. It lies dormant much of the winter, with activity picking up in late winter when the daylight hours increase.

As far as adaptability goes, the muskie is more sensitive to change than most game fish species. While tolerable to some species, changes in habitat, such as fertilizer runoff from farm fields or yards, flooding, or vegetation loss, can be devastating to muskie populations.

Spawning

The muskie's spawning activity is similar to the northern's, with a few differences. The muskie usually spawns later in the spring than the northern, though their spawning periods occasionally overlap. The muskie chooses a spawning ground in a shallow bay or a tributary stream. The peak of its spawning activity occurs when water temperatures have risen to between 48°F and 59°F (9°C and 15°C).

The female muskie reaches sexual maturity between the ages of four and six; the male is capable of spawning a year or two earlier in life. The female lays her eggs haphazardly like the northern, spreading them over a wide area—sometimes 100 yards (90 m) in length. Muskie eggs are nonadhesive, so they fall to the bottom. This sloppy spawning style results

Muskies' appearances vary from region to region. The three distinct versions of muskie markings at one time prompted biologists to classify the fish as three different species. One variation, common to Wisconsin, has dark bars on its sides. Another, which is most common in the northern and western parts of the muskie's range, has dark spots on its sides. Still another version, most often seen in the eastern part of the muskie's range, has virtually no markings on its sides. In the mid-twentieth century, ichthyologists discovered all three variations were the same fish. Photograph © Doug Stamm/ProPhoto

The tiger muskie is a northern pike and muskie hybrid. The fish do occur naturally, but more often fisheries managers manufacture tiger muskies in their hatcheries. While natural muskie plantings in waters outside their native range have been largely unsuccessful, the tiger muskie adapts well to habitats unacceptable to either parent. Today, tiger muskies are stocked in more than twenty-five states. Photograph © Patrice Ceisel/Shedd Aquarium

in a low fertilization rate. Although a female can lay as many as two hundred thousand eggs depending on her size, often only 30 percent become fertilized. The female usually spawns two times, with approximately two weeks between egg deposits.

The muskie eggs fortunate enough to be fertilized and survive predation hatch within one to two weeks. The fry feed on tiny zooplankton and invertebrates for the first few days of life, then in about one week they will eat fish, including other muskie fry. Many fry fall victim to larger fish; those that make it through the critical stages of early development grow to about 8 inches (20 cm) by the end of their first year.

TIGER MUSKIE

Named for the larger parent, the tiger muskie is actually a cross between a northern and a muskellunge. The hybridization does occur naturally, but some states and provinces breed tiger muskies for stocking because the crossbreed grows faster than muskies and tolerates higher water temperatures than either parent.

Although its growth rate and temperature tolerance are positive features, the species does have some drawbacks. The most significant negative is the hybrid's infertility, which makes it impossible to manage the tiger muskie as a self-sustaining species. A minor drawback is the tiger muskie's growth potential, which —often exceeding 30 pounds (14 kg)— does not approach that of the muskie.

The tiger muskie possesses physical traits of both parents. Its body usually bears dark bars on a light background like a muskie. The tips of its tail are rounded like the northern's. On each side of its lower jaw, the tiger muskie bears five to seven pores (a number that straddles the pore counts of its parental species).

CHAIN PICKEREL

Because it does not grow as large as the northern pike or muskie, the chain pickerel, *Esox niger*, receives far less attention from anglers. Named for the green chain-like pattern on its yellow-green side, the chain pickerel is sometimes confused with the northern. The chain pickerel, however, is a much smaller fish, with an average weight of 1 to 2 pounds (.45 to .9 kg). The world record caught by Baxley McCuaig, Jr. in 1961 in Homerville, Georgia, weighed 9 pounds, 6 ounces (4.25 kg). One way to distinguish it from the northern is to check the operacle, which is the main bone of the gill cover. The northern's operacle is scaled only on the upper half, whereas the chain pickerel's is completely scaled.

Found mainly on the East Coast, the chain pickerel's native range included the Atlantic drainages from Nova Scotia to Florida, and the southern Mississippi River drainages from Missouri to Louisiana. Transplantation expanded its range to include the drainages of Lake Erie and Lake Ontario, as well as various areas in the central United States.

The chain pickerel commonly lives in weedy lakes, the backwaters of rivers, and—occasionally—swamps, usually in 2 to 10 feet (.6 to 3 m) of water. Unlike the northern pike and muskie, the chain pickerel tolerates

water temperatures into the 80s (27°C to 32°C).

Like other *Esox* species, the chain pickerel eats mainly other fish, but also will prey on frogs, salamanders, crayfish, and mice.

Spawning

In early spring, right after ice-out, adult chain pickerel, which are those age two or older, move to their spawning grounds. Usually they select a shallow, marshy area in a lake or in the sluggish backwaters of a river or stream. The female deposits as many as thirty thousand adhesive eggs, which are fertilized by two or three males.

The eggs hatch in a period of one to two weeks. The fry spend their early days feeding on tiny plankton, and are soon ready to feed on larger food items such as other fish, insects, and worms.

GRASS AND REDFIN PICKEREL

The redfin pickerel, *Esox americanus americanus*, and the grass pickerel, *Esox americanus vermiculatus*, are the smallest members of the *Esocidae* family. Both average less than 1 pound (.45 kg). Their size severely limits their appeal as game fish, especially where their larger cousins, the

The redfin pickerel prefers a habitat of lakes, streams, swamps, and backwaters of rivers. It seeks high concentrations of aquatic plants and clean, silt-free water. It avoids high to moderate currents and open or deep water. Although the redfin pickerel rarely weighs more than 1 pound (.45 kg), it does put up a good fight on light tackle. Photograph © R. J. Goldstein/ Visuals Unlimited

northern pike or muskie, inhabit the same waters.

Although similar in appearance—with their long narrow bodies, dark bars on olive to brown sides, and white bellies—the two subspecies can be distinguished from one another in a couple of ways. The redfin, as its name indicates, has reddish lower fins and a reddish tail, while the grass pickerel's lower fins and tail are yellow-green. In addition, the redfin has a short, broad snout, while the grass pickerel's snout is long and narrow.

The redfin pickerel's range extends from southern Quebec to Florida, along the St. Lawrence and Atlantic drainages. The grass pickerel's range stretches from southeastern Manitoba to southern Quebec in the North, and from Louisiana to Alabama in the South. For the most part, the Appalachian Mountains are the dividing line between the redfin and the grass pickerels' ranges.

Like other *Esox* species, the redfin and grass pickerel prefer a habitat with dense vegetation. They commonly live in the shallow water of lakes and streams, in areas with heavy cover. The pickerels prey primarily on small fish, tadpoles, and worms, and may also feed on aquatic plants.

Both the redfin and grass pickerel spawn early in spring and occasionally again in the fall. They select a spawning area in shallow water where the females will lay as many as fifteen thousand eggs. Where the two species' ranges overlap, hybridization often occurs.

Chapter 8

TEMPERATE BASS

Renowned for their ravenous appetites, unmerciful fight, and cooperative attitudes toward taking a variety of baits, members of the temperate bass family have established a place near the top of our list of most popular game fish species. The four species found in North America's freshwaters each have a loyal following of anglers who enjoy the thrill of landing these hard-fighting fish. Their range is small compared to that of the widespread largemouth bass and walleye, yet temperate bass—especially the striped bass—continue to lure growing numbers of anglers to the waters they inhabit.

Temperate bass are true bass, unlike the improperly named black bass. Members of the family *Moronidae*, temperate bass bear no relation to black bass, which actually belong to the *Centrarchidae* or sunfish family. Some temperate bass are saltwater species, including the striped bass, which was once confined to the Atlantic Ocean and returned to freshwater only to spawn. Today, the striped bass calls an increasing number of inland waters home.

Each of the four temperate bass species found in North America's freshwaters—the striped bass, white bass, yellow bass, and white perch—share several characteristics: Their muscular bodies compress laterally and are fairly thick, each has a pair of dorsal fins with nine spines on the first and eleven to fourteen rays on the second, their mouths are relatively large and extend near or to the eye, and all but the white perch have a series of stripes running lengthwise along their sides.

Temperate bass live in a variety of waters, ranging from large, deep reservoirs

The white bass and its cousin the striped bass are the two most prevalent temperate bass species in the freshwaters of North America. The white bass's native range was limited mainly to the drainages of the Mississippi River, but extensive transplantation has expanded its range to nearly all of the contiguous forty-eight states, with the exception of a few in the east and northwest. Photograph © Doug Stamm/ProPhoto

to rivers to ponds. They prefer cooler water and avoid excessively warm lakes or rivers.

STRIPED BASS

Its size, strength, and tenacity have lifted the striped bass, *Morone saxatilis*, to an almost legendary position in the eyes of many anglers, making it without question the most popular of the temperate bass species. An average striper weighs about 8 pounds (3.6 kg), but 25-pound stripe bass (11-kg) are not uncommon, and a few have been caught weighing more than 50 pounds (23 kg).

The striped bass has a blue-gray to olive-brown back and six to nine gray stripes running lengthwise along each of its silver-white sides. The striper's mouth is large, extending to the eye, and the body is thick and bulky, especially in larger specimens.

The striper's successful introduction to North America's inland fresh-waters within the last thirty years parallels the chinook salmon's transplantation to the Great Lakes. Both species were originally anadromous fish that migrated up freshwater tributaries to spawn, and they have adapted well to inland freshwater.

The native range of the striper included the Atlantic Coast from New Brunswick to Florida, and the Gulf of Mexico Coast from Florida to Louisiana. Stocking extended its range to include much of the southern and eastern United States and the Pacific Coast.

Inland, the striper mainly lives in deep impoundments or rivers. Striped bass require cool water, preferably no higher than the mid-60s (17°C to 19°C); hot summer weather that raises water temperatures to 70°F (21°C) or higher is intolerable to the species. While the young can tolerate low oxygen levels, adult stripers require well-oxygenated water.

The adult stripers roam an impoundment or river in search of schools of baitfish or other food, such as mussels or worms. Their location in a given body of water often varies greatly from day to day as they move around in search of prey, trying to satisfy their voracious appetites. The creatures on which they feed are active during the night, thus most of the striper's feeding activity takes place under the cover of darkness.

The introduction of the striped bass to the inland fresh waters of the United States has created additional trophy fishing opportunities for countless anglers who do not have access to the fish's native coastal waters. The power, tenacity, beauty, and size of the striped bass make it one of North America's premier game fish. Photograph © Keith Sutton

Anadromous striped bass, which inhabit both the Atlantic and Pacific oceans, make their way up coastal tributaries to spawn in the spring. Whether living in an ocean or freshwater reservoir, schools of striped bass roam extensive areas in search of baitfish and other food. Anglers often find striped bass by locating areas with heavy baitfish activity. Photograph © Doug Stamm/ProPhoto

During the summer, stripers usually live in deep water, commonly 20 to 50 feet (5 to 15 m) down, where they remain until fall when they follow baitfish into shallow water. During the winter, the stripers move back out to deep water.

At sea, stripers live near river mouths, submerged structures, where currents meet, and other areas where baitfish congregate.

Spawning

Anadromous striped bass migrate to the mouths of large- to medium-sized rivers in spring for the spawn. The stripers congregate at the river mouths, waiting for the right conditions to move upstream. Usually, increased river flows from runoff and water temperatures in the 40s (4°C to 9°C) are the key ingredients.

Inland, the striper adapts to the conditions at hand. If it lives in a lake, a striper may spawn in a connecting river or in the shallows of the lake.

A female striper lays hundreds of thousands of eggs. The male fertilizes the eggs, then both parents abandon their offspring, leaving the eggs vulnerable to predators. Newly hatched fry form a school that sticks together for safety through much of their youth.

A note on the spawning activities of inland stripers: They often spawn with their cousins the white bass where the two species inhabit the same waters. The hybrid offspring are referred to as whiterock bass.

White Bass

A smaller yet popular freshwater cousin of the striped bass is the white bass, *Morone chrysops*. In many ways, the white bass bears a resemblance to a small striped bass. It has a blue-gray back and gray lines running lengthwise on its silver-white sides like the striper; however, the lines on white bass's sides tend to be broken. Also, the head dips inward from the nose to the back. The biggest distinction between the two species, though, is size: White bass grow nowhere near as large as the striper. The world record white bass, caught in 1989 by David Kraushaar in Saginaw Bay, Michigan, weighed 6 pounds, 7 ounces (2.92 kg); an average catch weighs closer to 1 pound (.45 kg).

The white bass's native range extended from eastern South Dakota to southern Quebec in the North, and from eastern New Mexico to Louisiana and western Mississippi in the South. Introduction expanded its range as far east as Georgia and South Carolina and to a few areas in the western United States.

Throughout its range, white bass live in schools in the fast, clean sections of rivers and in clear, deep lakes. During the daytime, the school, which is made up of similar-sized fish, lurks in deeper water, moving

Anglers can locate schools of white bass in the early morning and late evening feeding on schools of baitfish such as gizzard or threadfin shad, or hatches of insects. Unlike many of North America's game fish, the white bass does not hide in cover or stay in one specific area. It moves with the school, which continually moves with its food sources. Photograph © Doug Stamm/ ProPhoto

into shallow water to feed during the evening hours. Much of the white bass's popularity stems from the ease at which anglers can locate feeding schools. The fish feed heavily at the surface on baitfish such as gizzard shad or shiners, especially in late summer, and also will rise to the surface to take hatches of insects. A sure tip-off to the presence of white bass is a flock of gulls congregating near one of these feeding frenzies to pick up scraps.

Spawning

White bass spawn between the months of March and June, with the later spawn occurring in the northern latitudes of their range. By the time water temperatures reach between 55°F and 79°F (13°C and 26°C), white bass have migrated upriver or into tributary streams to spawn. For lake-dwellers, the spawn takes place in a tributary stream or near a shallow reef or bar. Males move to the spawning grounds well in advance of the females, usually when water temperatures are in the mid-40s (6°C to 8°C).

A female white bass lays hundreds of thousands of adhesive eggs, usually over gravel in shallow water. The male fertilizes the eggs, then both parents abandon the spawning site, moving downriver with the school.

The parents' lack of care for their young results in a high mortality rate in both eggs and fry. In about one week, the eggs that were fertilized—

The word mississippiensis *in the yellow bass's scientific name refers to the Mississippi River, where the fish was first discovered. The yellow bass's somewhat limited native range included mainly the Mississippi and a few nearby drainages, but transplantation has increased its distribution as far west as Arizona.* Photograph © Patrice Ceisel/Shedd Aquarium

Anglers often confuse young striped bass with white bass. One way to distinguish the two species is to check the gill covers: Two sharp points protrude from each of the striped bass's gill covers, while the white bass has only one point on each gill cover. Another identifying feature is dentition: The striped bass sports two patches of teeth on the back of its tongue, while the white bass is equipped with just one. Photograph © Patrice Ceisel/Shedd Aquarium

and that survived predation—hatch. The fry quickly school for safety. They feed on zooplankton and tiny crustaceans and grow 2 or 3 inches (5 to 7.5 cm) in the first year.

YELLOW BASS

Except for its yellow coloring, the yellow bass, *Morone mississippiensis*, is nearly identical to the white bass. The yellow bass has a green-gray back and silver-yellow sides, with rows of broken black stripes running lengthwise along its sides. The body features are similar to those of the white bass, though the yellow bass's mouth is not as large as its cousin's, and its two dorsal fins are connected. Yellow bass, though averaging about 1 pound (.45 kg), run a bit smaller than the white bass. While the record white bass weighed over 6 pounds (2.7 kg), the world record yellow bass, taken by Donald Stalker in 1977 in Lake Monroe, Indiana, weighed only 2 pounds, 4 ounces (1.02 kg).

The yellow bass's native range was limited mainly to the Mississippi

The yellow bass, like the white bass, moves in schools in search of aquatic insects, crustaceans, and small fish. Once anglers locate a group of yellow bass, they simply move with the school. Such a tactic usually results in a successful day on the water. Photograph © Keith Sutton

River drainages from Minnesota and Wisconsin south to Texas and Louisiana. It is also native to the Lake Michigan drainages of Wisconsin and Illinois, and the Mobile Bay drainages of Alabama and the western panhandle of Florida. Transplantation modestly distributed the yellow bass to other waters in the southern and southwestern United States.

Like the white bass, the yellow bass is a schooling fish that calls both rivers and lakes home. Unlike its cousin, though, the yellow bass spends most of its time in deep water near the bottom, rarely coming up to the surface to feed. Its diet consists mainly of minnows, aquatic insects, and crustaceans.

Spawning

The yellow bass's spawning activity is nearly identical to that of the white bass. Spawning takes place in the spring, between the months of March and June. The yellow bass adults select a spawning area in a tributary stream of rivers, or in shallow water in lakes. Neither parent makes a nest. The female just deposits her hundreds of thousands of eggs in a haphazard fashion over a gravel bottom. After the eggs are fertilized, both parents leave the spawning site and return to their schools.

WHITE PERCH

The smallest of the temperate bass is the white perch, *Morone americana*, which rarely grows larger than 3 pounds (1.4 kg). A more realistic catch weighs-in at about ½ pound (.23 kg). Similar in shape to white and yellow bass, the white perch lacks the distinct side stripes of its larger cousins. Its back is dark green, the sides are silver-green to blue-green, and the belly is white; colors, though, may vary considerably from one body of water to the next.

The native range of the white perch included the Atlantic Coast from southern Quebec to South Carolina, and stretched inland as far as Lake Ontario. Migration through the Erie Canal allowed the white perch to claim a home in Lake Erie and its drainages. Intentional and unintentional transplantation also expanded its range to more eastern waters.

The white perch mainly inhabits brackish waters of the coast, lakes, ponds, and the backwaters of rivers. Wherever it is found, white perch move in schools, feeding on aquatic insects, crustaceans, and small baitfish.

Spawning

Between April and June, adult white perch move into tributary streams to spawn in shallow water. When water temperatures reach the mid-50s (12°C to 14°C), the female deposits fifty thousand to one hundred thousand adhesive eggs at random, and the male fertilizes them. Both parents move away after spawning, leaving the eggs and fry to fend for themselves.

The eggs hatch in three to five days, and the fry school and feed on tiny zooplankton and other microorganisms.

Most often, white perch feed on small fish, crustaceans, or aquatic insects, but in the spring their focus may turn exclusively toward eating fish eggs. The eggs of game fish such as walleyes, sauger, and white bass face heavy losses from hungry schools of white perch keying in on the other fishes' spawning grounds. Photograph © Doug Stamm/ProPhoto

Chapter 9

STURGEON

Ancient, armored giants from a primitive era, sturgeon are the largest and oldest game fish species in North America. Prior to the late 1800s, sturgeon populations across the continent were high and healthy, but when international markets demanded sturgeon roe and flesh, populations suffered greatly. In some regions, sturgeon numbers were desperately depleted or even eradicated by years of commercial overfishing. Factors such as habitat loss from dam construction and pollution from industrial development also played key roles in thinning sturgeon populations. At one time, commercial anglers, who considered these odd-looking fish a nuisance species, systematically destroyed sturgeon. The good news for sturgeon and anglers alike is that populations slowly are beginning to rebound, thanks to the work of fisheries' managers and nonprofit organizations. Because of the fish's longevity, reestablishing sturgeon populations will be a long and arduous task. In the case of some species, it may take fifty years or more to see a marked improvement in populations.

The first time I laid eyes on a sturgeon, there was no question I was seeing a creature held over from a prehistoric time. Sturgeon, which date back to the Mesozoic era (65 to 230 million years ago), have long bodies that are scaleless, bearing instead rows of large bony plates on the back and sides called scutes. The head is shovel-shaped, with the mouth tucked far underneath. The tail has a

Found only in the largest rivers along the Pacific coast, the white sturgeon is the largest freshwater fish in North America, capable of growing in excess of 1,000 pounds (450 kg). During the nineteenth century, anglers used teams of mules to pull gigantic white sturgeon from the Columbia and Snake rivers in Washington. Reports from that period claim white sturgeon were responsible for the deaths of more than a few mule teams. Some of the most highly regarded white sturgeon waters include British Columbia's Fraser River; the Columbia, Willamette, and Snake rivers in Washington and Oregon; and the Sacramento-Joaquin system in California. Photograph © Keith Sutton

long upper tip, similar to that of a shark. Internally, the sturgeon's frame is a mix of cartilage and bone. The fish lacks a spinal column, instead possessing a white tubular column called a notochord, leftover from its primitive heritage.

The sturgeon is a bottom feeder and, like the catfish, possesses barbels that aid in the identification of prey. The four barbels located in front of the sturgeon's relatively small mouth are used to taste and feel food along the river or lake floor. When an object has been identified as food, the sturgeon sucks up the meal with its mouth. This meal often includes aquatic insects, worms, crayfish, small fish, leeches, snails, clams, and aquatic plants.

LAKE STURGEON

Although its populations suffered greatly from decades of overharvesting, the lake sturgeon, *Acipenser fulvescens*, remains the most common sturgeon species in North America's freshwaters and the most important game fish among sturgeons. The lake sturgeon's native range included an area stretching from Alberta to Quebec in the North, south through the Great Lakes region and the Mississippi River basin to Louisiana. Commercial overfishing and habitat loss extinguished lake sturgeon populations in parts of its southern range and depleted populations through much of the rest of its range. Management efforts are slowly bringing populations back in some areas. Today, quality lake sturgeon angling opportunities exist in Canada and through much of the Great Lakes region.

Reestablishing lake sturgeon populations is a slow process. Females, which sometimes live to age eighty, and in extreme cases live more than a century, may take up to twenty-three years to reach sexual maturity, and may only spawn every four to six years. Males, which have been known to live as long as fifty-five years or more, may not reach sexual maturity until age nineteen. This slow reproductive rate means fisheries'

Lake sturgeon are the most abundant sturgeon species in North America's freshwaters. During the late nineteenth and early twentieth centuries, overharvesting, pollution, and habitat loss had a devastating effect on their populations. Throughout much of the fish's range, management efforts have greatly improved populations, and lake sturgeon fishing is rising steadily in quality and popularity. Photograph © Patrice Ceisel/Shedd Aquarium

managers working on a lake sturgeon management project today may never see the outcome of their work.

The lake sturgeon is not the largest of the sturgeon species found in the North America, but it does grow to enormous sizes. On average, the fish weighs between 10 and 60 pounds (4.5 and 27 kg) and is capable of growing as large as 300 pounds (135 kg). The world record landed by Edward Paszkowski at the Nottawasage River in Ontario in 1982 weighed 168 pounds (76.20 kg).

An older lake sturgeon has a gray body and white belly, while a younger specimen tends to be more olive-brown above. The rows of scutes or plates running along the body are the same color as the skin.

As the name implies, lake sturgeon often inhabit lakes, but they also live in large rivers. They spend their time near the bottom, usually in water 15 feet (4.5 m) or more in depth and prefer fairly clear, cool water and a bottom of sand, gravel, or mud.

Spawning

Adult lake sturgeon congregate between May and June, depending on the latitude at which a population lives, to spawn in the deep holes of a lake or river. In frenzied anticipation, they roll near the bottom, a ritual that culminates in the fish breaking the surface or jumping out of the water.

The female lays her eggs, which total between five hundred thousand and two million, over an area of rock or gravel in fairly shallow water. One or more males fertilize the adhesive eggs, which stick to rocks or other submerged objects, such as plants or logs. When the adults complete the spawn, neither the male nor female remain behind to tend the eggs.

About one week after fertilization, the fry hatch. Measuring less than ½ inch (1.3 cm) in the first days of life, they grow quickly. By the end of the first year, they will have grown to more than 7 inches (18 cm) in length.

The young lake sturgeon is equipped with a suction cup on its snout that allows the fish to cling to rocks or other objects to rest in areas with high currents. When the fish reaches about 2 feet (60 cm) in length, it loses the suction cup.

White Sturgeon

The king of North America's freshwater game fish is the white sturgeon, *Acipenser transmontanus*. An average white sturgeon weighs-in at approximately 500 pounds (225 kg), but the fish is capable of growing to 1,400 pounds (630 kg). A British Columbia newspaper in 1897 reported that a netted white sturgeon weighed an estimated 1,800 pounds (810 kg). No white sturgeon in the four-digit weight class has ever been landed on rod and reel, but occasionally fish weighing more than 300 pounds (135 kg) are caught. Like most sturgeon species, its numbers were greatly depleted by overfishing and habitat loss. Recent management efforts have fared well, though, and white sturgeon numbers are

Around the beginning of the twentieth century, observers began noticing a significant depletion in white sturgeon populations after years of commercial overharvesting. Not until the 1950s did restrictive harvest regulations go in to effect in an attempt to save what remained of these mighty fish. By the 1970s, populations began to rebound, spurring a tremendous growth in the number of sport anglers pursuing white sturgeon. Photograph © Patrice Ceisel/Shedd Aquarium

beginning to rebound. States like Washington, Oregon and Idaho, which have implemented catch-and-release only regulations, have seen a gradual increase in numbers over the last twenty-five years.

The white sturgeon is gray to gray-brown on its upper body and white below, with light-colored scutes. Its barbels are located farther from its mouth than those of other sturgeon.

In many cases, white sturgeon live longer than humans. A ninety-year-old is not uncommon, and some have been known to live as long as 150 years.

The white sturgeon is generally an anadromous fish, living along the Pacific Coast from Alaska to California and extending inland as far as Idaho and extreme western Montana. Stocking efforts have brought populations to parts of the Colorado River. Landlocked white sturgeon occur in some areas, such as where dam construction has blocked their route to the sea. These landlocked populations seek holes, usually 30 to 70 feet (9 to 21 m) deep, away from strong current.

Spawning

The sea-run white sturgeon enters a large river in May or June, sometimes migrating hundreds of miles to reach its spawning ground. Landlocked whites move upriver to find their spawning grounds.

Most females reach sexual maturity between the ages of thirteen and sixteen, but for some, maturation takes more than twenty-five years. After spawning, they may take up to eleven years off between spawning trips. The male is usually capable of spawning at age ten or eleven, but again, maturation takes considerably longer in some cases. The male returns to spawn in intervals of about five years.

The females deposit as many as four million eggs in areas with a gravel bottom and moderate water flow, and the male fertilizes the eggs. The eggs adhere to the rocks and hatch in about one week.

ATLANTIC STURGEON

Commercial overfishing, pollution, and dam construction have devastated populations of Atlantic sturgeon, *Acipenser oxyrhynchus*. Throughout much of its current range—including the Atlantic Coast from Labrador to northern Florida, and the Gulf of Mexico Coast from northern Florida to Louisiana—the Atlantic sturgeon is protected by strict limits and short seasons. Angling opportunities are limited and rarely taken advantage of, but those who do pursue the Atlantic sturgeon hope to hook North America's second-largest game fish. An average Atlantic tips the scales at about 150 pounds (68 kg), but is capable of growing as large as 800 pounds (360 kg), and living as long as seventy years.

One key identifying feature of the Atlantic sturgeon is its long, narrow snout, which turns upward in younger specimens and draws to a distinctive V-shape. The body is blue-black to green-black with darker coloring on the back and lighter coloring on the sides. It has a white belly and white spines on the scutes.

Spawning

The Atlantic sturgeon is anadromous. Except for the early years, it spends most of its life in the ocean, returning to tributaries only to spawn. Spawning adults migrate to the rivers in the spring and can travel incredible distances to reach the spawning grounds. Some Atlantics travel as far as 900 miles (1,440 km). Males, who reach sexual maturity between the

During the 1990s, most states along the Atlantic coast closed their Atlantic sturgeon fishing seasons in an attempt to improve the fish's populations, which had been hit hard by commercial overharvesting, pollution, and habitat loss. Atlantic sturgeon spawn in more than thirty rivers between Maine and Florida, with the highest populations found in the Hudson River. Photograph © Rob & Ann Simpson

ages of ten and fourteen, move into the river first; females, who may not reach sexual maturity until age nineteen, follow. When the adults arrive at the spawning grounds, the female deposits as many as two million eggs over an area with a moving current and a gravel bottom, then one or more males fertilize the eggs. When spawning is complete, both parents abandon the eggs. The female returns to the ocean almost immediately, while the male commonly remains in the river until fall.

The adhesive eggs stick to the gravel bottom, where they incubate for one or two weeks before hatching. The young Atlantic sturgeon usually stay in the river three to five years before moving out to the ocean, though sometimes they remain in freshwater as long as seven years.

SHOVELNOSE STURGEON

Although its size limits its attraction as a game fish, the shovelnose sturgeon, *Scaphirhynchus platorynchus*, has excellent tasting meat and provides an admirable fight on light tackle. An average shovelnose weighs about 2 pounds (.9 kg), but the fish is capable of growing in excess of 7 pounds (3.2 kg). Three or four generations of shovelnose sturgeon, which rarely live beyond fifteen years, may pass during the life of a single lake or white sturgeon.

As its name implies, the shovelnose carries a flat, shovel-shaped head. From the head, its back rises to a gradual hump then tapers to a long, thin tail. The body is brown throughout, except for the white belly, which has scutes on its surface.

Shovelnose populations remain relatively stable through much of its range, which includes the Mississippi River basin from Montana to western Pennsylvania in the North and from Texas to Alabama in the South. Populations are highest in the northern sections of the fish's range. The shovelnose prefers a habitat of fast-moving water, and commonly lives near dams, rapids, or other areas of high flow, in large- to medium-sized rivers.

The shovelnose sturgeon uses its long barbels to comb the river bottom for food. It lives in areas with high populations of clams and snails, which are among its preferred prey. It also feeds heavily on aquatic insects, such as caddisfly larvae and dragonfly nymphs, and a variety of aquatic plants. Photograph © Keith Sutton

Spawning

In May or June, adults migrate upstream or into smaller tributaries to spawn. Females reach sexual maturity around age seven; males usually are ready to spawn by their fifth year. A female may lay more than fifty thousand adhesive eggs, which stick to rocks and other submerged objects.

Shovelnose fry grow to about 2 inches (5 cm) in their first year. They live in or near the main channel, feeding on plankton and aquatic insects.

The shovelnose sturgeon commonly lives over sand or gravel in deep river channels with high current. Throughout its native waters of the Mississippi River and its tributaries, anglers often locate shovelnose sturgeon in the heavy current below dams. Rarely are these ancient fish found in quiet water. The pallid sturgeon, which bears a close resemblance to the shovelnose, shares much of the same habitat and food with its cousin. Originally considered a shovelnose, ichthyologists recategorized the pallid sturgeon as a distinct species in 1905. In 1990, the pallid sturgeon was added to the federal endangered species list. Today, states throughout its range are working to bring its populations back, so one day anglers can again enjoy pallid sturgeon fishing. Photograph © Rob & Ann Simpson

In contrast to most other sturgeon species, the meat of a green sturgeon is not highly regarded by anglers or cooks. Green sturgeon meat is usually reddish in color and has an offensive taste and smell, one reason the fish has never gained popularity among sport or commercial fishermen and women. Photograph © Daniel W. Gotshall

GREEN STURGEON

Another anadromous West Coast sturgeon is the green sturgeon, *Acipenser medirostris.* Commonly passed over by anglers who prefer the larger white sturgeon, the green sturgeon carries little weight as a game fish. Although it may grow in excess of 300 pounds (135 kg), an average green sturgeon will weigh well under 100 pounds (45 kg).

The green sturgeon is named for its green skin, making it easily identifiable. The back and sides are dark to light green, and the belly is greenish-white. Some specimens in the northern regions of the fish's range have green stripes on their undersides.

The green sturgeon's range is similar to that of the white sturgeon, stretching along the Pacific Coast from Alaska to California. Adults live in the ocean and migrate into large rivers to spawn, but do not travel as far inland as the white sturgeon.

PALLID STURGEON

Closely resembling the shovelnose, the pallid sturgeon, *Scaphirhynchus albus,* lives mainly in the Missouri River from Montana, south through the Lower Mississippi River to Louisiana. In some areas the two species' ranges overlap. The pallid's shorter barbels, larger head, smaller eyes, and a lack of scutes on the belly help anglers distinguish it from the shovelnose. It also is lighter in color, with a gray to bluish-gray body and white underside. The pallid sturgeon is capable of growing much larger than its cousin. The world record, caught by Robert C. Carlson at the Missouri River in North Dakota in 1984, weighed-in at 49 pounds, 8 ounces (22.45 kg). More typically though, the pallid weighs less than 15 pounds (6.8 kg).

The pallid sturgeon prefers a habitat within the strong flow of a river's main channel over a bottom of gravel or sand. Like the shovelnose, it migrates into tributaries to spawn in mid- to late spring.

Chapter 10

SHAD

O n both the Atlantic and Pacific Coasts of North America, shad spawning runs are events of terrific proportion, paralleled only by the salmon runs of the Pacific Coast. The banks of celebrated shad-filled rivers, like the Connecticut and Delaware endure hordes of elbow-to-elbow anglers, each drifting and jigging for these highly prized fish. Festivals often accompany the runs in communities near the most popular shad rivers.

Shad belong to family *Clupeidae*, which also includes herrings. The American and hickory shad are the largest members of the shad and herring family and are valued game fish. Smaller cousins such as the gizzard shad and threadfin shad play important roles as food sources for numerous game fish species.

The American and hickory shad spend the majority of their lives in the ocean, returning to coastal tributaries to spawn. Other shad, such as the gizzard and threadfin, are native to inland freshwaters.

~&~

American shad spend most of their lives in the ocean, becoming available to freshwater anglers along the Atlantic and Pacific coasts only during the spring, when the spawning fish migrate up tributary streams. Indigenous to the Atlantic Coast, American shad were transplanted to the West coast. One of the heaviest American shad runs occurs in Washington's Columbia River, where an estimated four million or more fish enter the river each year. Photograph © Doug Stamm/ProPhoto

AMERICAN SHAD

The largest and most popular member of the shad and herring family is the American shad, *Alosa sapidissima*. The world record weighed-in at more than 11 pounds (5 kg), far surpassing the maximum size limits of its smaller cousins. More commonly, anglers hook American shad weighing in the neighborhood of 2 to 4 pounds (.9 to 1.8 kg).

In the late nineteenth and early twentieth centuries, the American shad played a more important role as a commercial species than as a game fish. In the years following World War II, its popularity exploded as more and more anglers discovered the sport value of this feisty, tasty fish.

The American shad, which has a distinctly compressed green to blue body with silvery sides, can be identified by its single, evenly rounded dorsal fin. The species is also identifiable by its long jaw, which extends well beyond the eyes. Other characteristics include two dark spots above the gill cover, followed by three to four smaller spots, a deeply forked tail, and a soft mouth. The American shad does not have scales on its head, or a lateral line.

Prior to the late 1800s, the American shad's range included the Atlantic Coast from Labrador to Florida. In the 1870s, the fish was introduced to the Pacific Coast and gradually staked out a western range stretching from Alaska to Mexico.

Heavy commercial netting in the late nineteenth and early twentieth centuries took a toll on American shad populations. Also, as development and industry increased along the coasts, pollution and dams ruined a great deal of habitats and hit the species' populations hard. The good news is that conservation efforts aimed at improving habitats and increasing shad populations have had a positive effect in recent years, and are helping to ensure quality American shad angling opportunities for future generations.

The majority of the American shad's life is spent in the ocean. In many regions, schools of American shad may migrate more than one thousand miles (1,600 km) in a year. A school's movement in the ocean is driven by the search for food and, toward spring, the drive to reproduce. The American shad's major food source is plankton; its diet also includes insects, shrimp, and small fish.

Spawning

Depending on the region, schools of American shad make their spawning runs between winter and early summer, with the later runs occurring in the northern latitudes. Like salmon, shad return to the river in which they hatched, congregating at the mouths of the tributaries until conditions are right to make the move upstream. Usually tributary water temperatures rising to the low- to mid-50s (10°C to 14°C) trigger the migration.

Migrating shad, whose colors take on a beautiful, iridescent tone, follow the main channel of the river upstream. In some rivers, the fish travel more than 30 miles (48 km) a day and migrate hundreds of miles

American shad, like other shad species, are schooling fish. In the ocean, schools move up and down the coast in search of food. They even make their migrating run upstream as a school, a phenomena that makes spawning runs easy for anglers to locate. The hickory shad, which looks very much like the American shad, migrates up many of the same Atlantic coast tributaries as its cousin. Although they are similar in appearance and share common migratory routes, when found together, the larger American shad attracts more attention from anglers. Photograph © Doug Stamm/ProPhoto

Gizzard shad undergo significant physical changes as they grow. A young gizzard shad has teeth on its tongue to help it eat various crustaceans and aquatic insects, but loses the teeth later in life as the fish settles into a diet almost exclusively of aquatic plants. Like the American shad, young gizzard shad have shoulder spots, which often fade as they grow. Photograph © Mark Giovanetti/ProPhoto

to reach the spawning grounds. Males, which reach sexual maturity at age three or four, arrive at the spawning grounds first. The females, which are capable of spawning at age five or six, follow a week or two later. Spawning typically takes place at night, when water temperatures are between 60°F and 70°F (16°C and 21°C). Neither male nor female builds a nest for the eggs; rather, the female deposits the eggs, which can number as many as six hundred thousand, at random in shallow water. The male then fertilizes the eggs, which are nonadhesive and float with the current.

In an odd quirk of nature, spawning American shad in the southern ranges commonly perish after spawning, while their cousins in the northern ranges usually survive the migratory run and return to spawn again.

Due to the sloppy spawning practices of the American shad, the mortality rate of eggs is high. The eggs that are fertilized and survive predation and other hazards hatch in about one week. The fry school and feed heavily on tiny zooplankton for the duration of the summer. In the fall, when they are about 5 inches (13 cm) long, the young fish move out to the ocean where they remain until their time comes to make the spawning run.

HICKORY SHAD

A smaller version of the American shad, the hickory shad, *Alosa mediocris*, cannot compete with its much larger cousin in size. The world record hickory shad, caught by Ralph Dan Johnson in 1992 in Tar River, North Carolina, weighed a mere 3 pounds, 8 ounces (1.59 kg). An average hickory shad weighs closer to 1 pound (.45 kg).

Colored green to green-gray above and silver below, the hickory shad's body compresses strongly from the sides. A blue-black spot sits above the gill cover, followed by a row of four or five smaller, less defined spots. One characteristic that sets it apart from the American shad is the row of faint stripes running lengthwise along each of the hickory's sides. The hickory has a large jaw that extends beyond the middle of its eyes. The lower jaw, which is equipped with small teeth, sticks out in an exaggerated under bite. Like the American shad, the hickory has just one dorsal fin and a forked tail, but the hickory shad's tail forks more deeply than its cousin's.

The hickory shad's range includes the Atlantic Coast from northern Maine to northern Florida. It shares habitats with the American shad in many areas, but the two species do not necessarily share the same food sources. While the American shad feeds mainly on plankton, the hickory depends more on baitfish for sustenance, feeding heavily on eels, small fish, squid, and crabs.

Spawning

Although the hickory shad's range extends as far north as Maine, the spring spawning runs into coastal tributaries occur almost exclusively south of the Chesapeake Bay. Why northern hickories do not migrate up coastal rivers is unclear.

Hickories that do make the spawning run into the tributaries begin moving upstream between May and June, depending on the latitude and weather. Like the American shad, hickories follow the main channel of the river on their journey to the spawning grounds. Females deposit their eggs in a haphazard fashion in shallow water, and the males move in to fertilize them. Neither parent provides care for the eggs, which are nonadhesive and float helplessly with the current.

Once hatched, the hickory fry form a school and feed heavily on tiny plankton to gain strength and size for their journey to the ocean.

GIZZARD SHAD

Although it most often plays the role of prey for numerous game fish species, the gizzard shad, *Dorosoma cepedianum*, also provides sport fishing action for a limited number of anglers in the eastern half of the United States. Inhabiting lakes and rivers in a range stretching from North Dakota to southern Quebec in the North and New Mexico to Florida in the South, the gizzard shad is nearly always found in freshwater, though it is known to enter brackish water along the Atlantic and Gulf Coasts.

The gizzard shad resembles both the American and hickory shad, but it has a few distinguishing features. The most notable is a long, whip-like ray that hangs off the rear of the dorsal fin. A single, purple spot sits above each gill cover and its silvery-blue back and white sides are crossed by six to eight dark stripes. The gizzard shad averages less than 1 pound (.45 kg), but the world record, caught by Richard "Slim" Rutschkue in the Missouri River in South Dakota in 1992, tipped the scales at 4 pounds, 6 ounces (1.98 kg).

Water temperature plays a significant role in the American shad's movements during the year. At sea the fish seeks temperatures in a range between 45 to 55° F (8 to 13° C). In the late winter, spring, or early summer, American shad start moving into tributaries for their spawning run when water temperatures are between 50 to 55° F (10 to 13° C). The spawn takes place when the water warms to between 55 to 68° F (13 to 20° C). Whether at sea or in a river, the American shad avoids water temperatures below 45° F (8° C). Photograph © Doug Stamm/ProPhoto

CONSERVING OUR FISHERIES

The future of angling in North America depends greatly upon the actions and ethics of today's anglers. This continent's game fish species are a finite and fragile resource. Fortunately, fisheries' managers, nonprofit organizations, and anglers are quickly discovering the benefits of regulations, such as catch-and-release and slot limits, which protect our fisheries and help them grow and flourish. Passing new laws to protect fish is only the first step, though, because no matter how many rules and regulations a state's or province's department of natural resources establishes, the regulations will not work unless anglers are willing to abide by them and share responsibility in maintaining our fisheries.

Long before special regulations became popular, trout anglers learned that practicing catch-and-release helps maintain a fishery, produces larger fish, and gives other anglers a chance at catching trophy-trout. Muskie, northern, and bass anglers, among others, have adopted these practices as well. Today, catch-photo-and-release angling is replacing catch-and-kill in many angling circles. No one is suggesting that a few fish cannot be taken home for dinner. The point is, angling responsibly and not abusing the resources will help keep fisheries productive and healthy, especially with the growing number of anglers pressuring our continent's rivers, streams, and lakes.

Of course, no regulations can help protect game fish species if their habitats become tainted or destroyed. Negative outside influences, such as pollution and development, are constantly endangering our fisheries. The only way these resources can be protected is for anglers to become actively involved in preserving existing

North America's lakes, rivers, and streams—and the fish that inhabit them—are a finite resource. They are fragile and precarious treasures with fates dependent on the actions of humans. Countless waters and their game fish populations have been lost already to sport fishing through careless disregard for our natural resources. If generations living one hundred years from now are to enjoy the tremendous angling experienced by today's fishermen and women, then the current generation of anglers must set the foundation for continued vigilance in protecting our continent's freshwaters. Photograph © Rob & Ann Simpson

habitats and restoring damaged waters. Not everyone has to be an active lobbyist or help clean up a river. Joining a nonprofit organization that is active in lobbying, keeping a watchful eye over the game fish waters near home, or picking up a beer can floating in a lake are little, but important, ways anglers can help. If everyone does their part, North America's freshwater fisheries will remain a shining, priceless resource future generations can enjoy and cherish.

The number of people fishing on North America's lakes, rivers, and streams increases steadily with each new year, meaning greater pressure is being applied to the continent's game fish, which are a fragile and finite resource. Anglers who practice catch-photo-and-release help to minimize that pressure and preserve our fisheries for future generations. Photograph © Richard Hamilton Smith

Hooked largemouth bass often break water while trying to shake free from an angler's bait. The tactic works well, as more than a few anglers have lost a largemouth when the fish cleared the water in an acrobatic display of defiance and desperation. Photograph © Jack Bissell

The rugged and scenic beauty of the Yellowstone River draws anglers from throughout the world, who long to live the dream of landing colorful trout in front of the river's wild and picturesque backdrop. The Yellowstone is one of the most renowned trout waters on the continent, holding exceptional populations of rainbow, cutthroat, and other trout. Photograph © George Robbins Photo

BIBLIOGRAPHY

Al Linder's Outdoors. *Pike*. Brainerd, Minn.: Al Linder's Outdoors, 1990.

Becker, George C. *Fishes of Wisconsin*. Madison: University of Wisconsin Press, 1986.

Breining, Greg. *Managing Minnesota's Fish*. St. Paul, Minn.: Minnesota DNR, Section of Fisheries, 1989.

Calabi, Silvio. *Game Fish of North America*. Secaucus, N.J.: Wellfleet Press, 1988.

In-Fisherman. *Largemouth Bass in the 1990s*. Brainerd, Minn.: In-Fisherman, 1992.

Koller, Larry. *The Treasury of Angling*. New York: Golden Press, 1963.

McClane, A. J., ed. *McClane's New Standard Fishing Encyclopedia and International Angling Guide*. New York, N.Y.: Holt, Rinehart and Winston, 1974.

Netherby, Steve, ed. *The Expert's Book of Freshwater Fishing*. New York: Simon and Schuster, 1974.

Page, Lawrence M., and Brooks M. Burr. *A Field Guide to Freshwater Fishes*. Boston: Houghton Mifflin, 1991.

Parsons, P. Allen. *Outdoor Life Complete Book of Freshwater Fishing*. New York: Outdoor Life Books, 1963.

Schultz, Ken, and Dan D. Gapen. *The Complete Book of Freshwater Fishing*. Lexington, Mass.: S. Greene Press/Pelham Books, 1989.

Walden, Howard T. *Familiar Freshwater Fishes of America*. New York: Harper & Row, 1964.

Weidensaul, Scott. *The Freshwater Fish Identifier*. New York: Mallard Press, 1992.

Wisner, Bill. *The Fishermen's Sourcebook*. New York: Macmillan, 1983.

INDEX

ABOUT THE AUTHOR

Photograph © David Sorenson

$\mathcal{E}$ric L. Sorenson, an award-winning sports editor and outdoors writer, based in the Minneapolis–St. Paul area, began fishing thirty years ago as a child, exploring the pristine lakes of northern Minnesota and the Twin Cities with his grandfather.

Sorenson, who earned his bachelor of arts degree from the University of Minnesota's School of Journalism and Mass Communications, has contributed his freelance articles to outdoors magazines such as *In-Fisherman, Walleye In-Sider, Mid West Outdoors,* and *Outdoor News.* When not writing, he is most commonly found on a trout stream; he also fishes for trophy muskies, walleyes, panfish, steelhead, and salmon.

The Angler's Guide to Freshwater Fish of North America is his first book.